# TURKEY

## A PRIMARY SOURCE CULTURAL GUIDE

Martha Kneib

The Rosen Publishing Group's
PowerPlus Books™
New York

*To Tilly,*
*you were very little but you leave a big hole in our hearts*

Published in 2004 by The Rosen Publishing Group, Inc.
29 East 21st Street, New York, NY 10010

First Edition

### Library of Congress Cataloging-in-Publication Data
Kneib, Martha.
Turkey : a primary source cultural guide / Martha Kneib.— 1st ed.
   p. cm. — (Primary sources of world cultures)
Summary: An overview of the history and culture of Turkey and its people including the geography, myths, arts, daily life, education, industry, and government, with illustrations from primary source documents.
Includes bibliographical references and index.
ISBN 0-8239-3842-5 (alk. paper)
1. Turkey—Juvenile literature. [1. Turkey.]
I. Title. II. Series.
DR417 .K59 2003
956.1—dc21
                                                                                    2002015438

*Manufactured in the United States of America*

**Cover images:** The Codex Justinianus (background); the Hagia Sophia (middle); and musicians from the Ottoman Mehter marching band (bottom).

**Photo credits:** cover (background), pp. 81, 82 © Art Archive; cover (middle), pp. 73, 116 (left), 118 (second from top) © Paul Hardy/Corbis; cover (bottom), pp. 5 (top and middle), 19, 55, 56, 59, 78, 87, 88, 95, 96, 110, 116 (right) © AP/Wide World Photos; pp. 3, 118 (map), 120 © 2002 GeoAtlas; pp. 4 (top), 8, 33, 90, 92, 98 © Jeffrey Alford/Asia Access; pp. 4 (middle), 28 (top) © 2000 N. Carter/Northwind Picture Archives; pp. 4 (bottom), 22, 26 (bottom), 46, 52 © AKG London; pp. 5 (bottom), 102, 106 © Phyllis Picardi/International Stock; p. 6 © Eitan Simanor/Axiom; p. 7 © Bill Gleasner/Viesti & Associates, Inc.; pp. 9, 13, 14, 18 © Robert Frerck/Woodfin Camp & Associates; p. 10 © Edmund Nagele/International Stock; pp. 11, 51, 97 © Jeff Greenberg/Photri Inc.; p. 12 © Adam Woolfitt/Woodfin Camp & Associates; p. 15 © R&S Michaud/Woodfin Camp & Associates; p. 16 © Fred Maroon/Photo Researchers, Inc.; p. 17 © Lawrence Manning/Corbis; p. 20 © A.S.K./Viesti & Associates, Inc.; pp. 23, 57, 60, 67 © Archivo Iconografico, S.A./Corbis; pp. 24, 32 (bottom), 36 © The Granger Collection; pp. 25, 45 © Corbis; pp. 26 (top), 37, 42 (top) © Dorling Kindersley; p. 27 © Bridgeman Art Library; p. 28 (bottom), 40, 62 © Giraudon/Art Resource; p. 29 (top) © Topham/Art Resource; pp. 29 (bottom), 38 (bottom) © Werner Forman/Art Resource; pp. 30, 74, 77, 101 © Chris Hellier/Corbis; p. 31 © Library of Congress; pp. 32 (top), 34 © Bettmann/Corbis; p. 35 © AFP; p. 38 (top) © Walter Bibikow/The Viesti Collection; p. 39 (top) © Mansell/TimePix; p. 39 (bottom) © The Pierpont Morgan Library/Art Resource; p. 42 (bottom) © Jeff Greenberg/Photo Researchers, Inc.; p. 43 courtesy of the Cultural and Tourism Office of the Turkish Embassy; p. 44 © Chris Lisle/Corbis; p. 48 © Gilles Mermet/AKG London; p. 49 © British Library/AKG London; pp. 54, 111 © Reuters NewMedia Inc./Corbis; p. 58 © C. Refik Ongan/DiaStore; p. 61 © David Lees/Corbis; p. 64 © Brown Brothers; pp. 65 (top), 118 (second from bottom) © Josef Polleross/The Image Works; p. 65 (bottom) © Topham/The Image Works; p. 68 © Hans Georg Roth/Corbis; p. 69 © Richard T. Nowitz/Corbis; pp. 70, 79, 118 (bottom) © National Geographic; p. 71 © The Image Works; p. 72 © Woodfin Camp & Associates; pp. 75, 118 (top) © Yann Arthus-Bertrand/Corbis; p. 80 © Dagli Orti/Topkapi Museum Istanbul/Art Archive; pp. 84, 85, 86 © Iletisim Yayinlari; pp. 91, 93 © Snowdon/Hoyer/Woodfin Camp & Associates; pp. 99, 109 © Roberto Arakaki/International Stock; p. 100 © Jeffrey L. Rotman/Corbis; p. 103 © Karen Huntt Mason/Corbis; p. 104 © David Rubinger/Corbis; p. 105 © Steffan Widstrand/Corbis; p. 107 © Richard T. Nowitz/Photri Inc.; p. 108 © Photri Inc.; p. 121 © Farrell Grehan/Corbis.

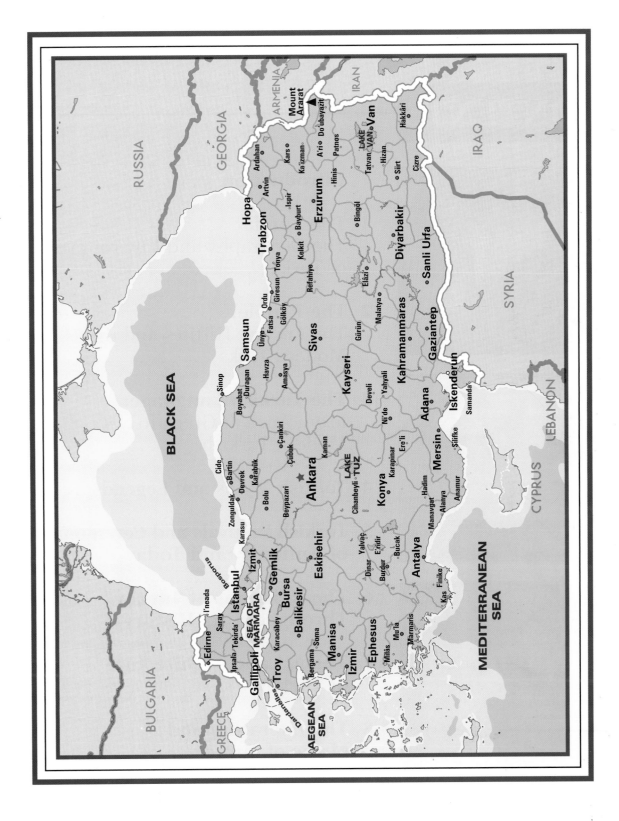

# CONTENTS

# INTRODUCTION

Turkey is a fascinating country that is a mix of ancient and modern cultures. Its geography has made Turkey one of the world's natural crossroads, paving the way for a long history of ambitious conquerors and grand empires.

Turkey lies between two continents: Europe and Asia. The Asian region is known as Anatolia, while the European region is called Thrace. Separating the two continents is the Sea of Marmara, and two straits: the Dardanelles and the Bosporus.

Even today, myths and legends about the Turks and their cities are often familiar. Jason traveled through the Bosporus to the Black Sea to find the Golden Fleece. The Greeks came to Anatolia to battle with the people of the fabled city of Troy. Heroes like Jason, Achilles, Aeneas, Ajax, and Hercules fought their enemies, followed their dreams, and sometimes died on the fertile land of Anatolia.

The Hittites, a Bronze Age people who spoke an Indo-European language, were the first civilization to prosper in Anatolia. After the Hittites came the Persians, the Greeks, the Romans, and the Turks. Each of these cultures contributed to the history, religion, art, and architecture of modern Turkey.

Constructed by Council Gaius Julius Aguila in AD 110, the Celsus Library *(left)* in the historical city of Ephesus, Turkey, once held approximately 12,000 handwritten scrolls. Along with literature, this library displayed statues of Roman goddesses now housed at Vienna's Ephesus Museum. Early in the seventeenth century, Sedefkar Mehmet Agha built the Sultanahmet Mosque *(above)* in Istanbul. However, its more common name is the Blue Mosque because of its blue stenciled designs.

The ruins of the Sumela Monastery sit 3,937 feet (1,200 meters) above sea level on Zigana Mountain. Greek monks first established the monastery in the fourteenth century around what they believed to be an icon of the Virgin Mary.

The first Turks who came to Anatolia were the Seljuk Turks. They arrived as mamluks, or slave soldiers, to the Samanid rulers of Persia, now present-day Iran. During the thirteenth century, the Ottoman Turks under Osman displaced the Seljuks and destroyed the Byzantine Empire in 1453.

The Ottoman Turks imported learning from the Muslim empires to the east, as well as the Persian language, which was the language of poetry, literature, and official court functions. They built impressive monuments like Topkapi Palace, and within one hundred years of defeating Constantinople (Istanbul), they had marched nonstop over much of Europe until they reached the gates of Vienna.

The nineteenth and twentieth centuries saw the decline of the Ottoman Empire, until it finally crumbled completely in 1918 after World War I. Young Turkish intellectuals tried to reform the government from within, but their efforts failed. Yet Mustafa Kemal, known as Atatürk, who was president of Turkey from 1923 to 1938, managed to institute progressive reforms in the nation. He imposed new suffrage

laws that gave women the right to vote. He stressed education for all Turks, including women, who, previous to his leadership, were discouraged from seeking an education. Traditional forms of dress were discouraged. Most of all, Atatürk wanted to lead Turkish citizens away from the older Ottoman Islamic customs. Daily life was overturned for most Turks when Atatürk transformed his country into one that more accurately reflected twentieth-century values.

Not everything has gone smoothly for Turkey since Atatürk's reforms. The government has been overthrown by military coups on several occasions. Economic reform has lagged in recent years, and the Turkish lira has lost value. Still, the spirit of reform thrives, and Turks continue to bring their nation beyond Atatürk's vision to greet the twenty-first century.

Istanbul, now a modern, industrial city with a rising populace, has served as an important landmark throughout Turkey's history. Each siege of the city brought a new name: New Rome, Second Rome, Byzantium, Constantinople, and finally Istanbul in 1453, when it was the seat of the Ottoman Empire.

# THE LAND

## The Geography and Environment of Turkey

Turkey occupies both the European and Asian continents. The Asian region, which is larger, is called Anatolia, or Asia Minor. The European region is known as Thrace. Together, these territories occupy more than 301,382 square miles (780,579 square kilometers). Turkey is about the size of Texas and Ohio combined.

## Anatolia

Anatolia is bounded on its western border by the Aegean Sea, and in the south partly by the Mediterranean, a waterway known as the Akdeniz, or "White Sea" in Turkish. In the north, Anatolia is bordered by the Black Sea, or Karadeniz. Its land boundaries span several countries, including Syria, Iraq, Iran, Georgia, Azerbaijan, and Armenia. Most of Anatolia—nearly 80 percent—is composed of the Central Plateau, surrounded by mountains where farming is sometimes difficult. The Aegean coast of Anatolia is made up of lowlands that are much more fertile than the Central Plateau. This area gets ample rain, and more than half of Turkey's crops are grown in this region. To the south, near the Mediterranean Sea, Turkey's soil is also rich for

Calcium carbonate deposits from hot springs give Pamukkale *(left)* its name, meaning the "Cotton Fortress." Cappadocia *(above)* is sometimes referred to as the Land of the Fairy Chimneys since many of its natural rock formations have a conical-shaped body with a boulder on top. Between the fourth and fourteenth centuries, Cappadocia housed a large community of Christian monks, who dutifully carved decorated dwelling spaces for as many as 30,000 worshipers.

growing crops. This area commonly produces a variety of citrus fruits as well as grapes. To the north, on the Black Sea coast, many Turks make their living as commercial fishermen.

## Cappadocia

One of the most geographically interesting places in Turkey is located in Anatolia and was created naturally. Volcanic eruptions in Cappadocia left soft layers of volcanic rock that have since eroded and created small mounds of rock known as fairy chimneys. Even more unusual are the underground cities that lie beneath Cappadocia. More than 2,000 years old and dating back to the Byzantine Empire, these large underground cities unfold into a series of tunnels, rooms, and narrow channels that may run at least 6 miles (8.4 kilometers) underground. It is believed that the underground city could have held

Aydintepe Village *(left)* is located in eastern Anatolia, known to Turks as the Land of the Mother Son. Karanlik Kilise, or "Dark Church," *(above)* is one of many churches carved out of rock by Christians during the later part of the eleventh century. These churches are still accessible to tourists as part of the Göreme Open Air Museum in the Cappadocia region.

as many as 25,000 people and was created for the purposes of defense, or for Christians who were hiding from persecution.

## A Mountainous Region

Although it is primarily mountainous, Turkey supports a wide range of climates. It produces many different crops and supports a variety of livestock and fishing industries. The Taurus Mountains at the south of the Central Plateau separate its lowlands along the Mediterranean Sea. Some of these mountains reach heights of 10,000 feet (3,050 meters). Other mountain chains in the far eastern part of Turkey extend even higher. The tallest mountain in Turkey, Mount Agri Dagi, which is also known as Mount Ararat, is approximately 16,946 feet (5,165 meters) high. Many of Turkey's mountains are extinct volcanoes. A few of them have lakes in their inactive craters. Other lakes in the region, like Van Gölü, or Lake Van, occupy depressions in the lava fields surrounding these extinct volcanoes. Lake Van is nearly the size of the U.S. state of Rhode Island.

# Thrace

Unlike Anatolia, Thrace is a much smaller region of Turkey. Its importance, however, is not diminished by its overall area, especially since Istanbul, the capital of the Ottoman Empire, is located there. Thrace is bounded by Bulgaria and Greece, as well as by the Black and Aegean Seas. Because Istanbul, and before that Constantinople, controlled the narrow bodies of water that separate Europe from Asia, Thrace has been strategically important for thousands of years.

The Gallipoli peninsula is another important natural and strategic component of Thrace. In 1915, during the First World War, Gallipoli was where the Allies tried to defeat the Ottoman Empire that supported Germany.

Armies and merchants have ferried their men and supplies across its straits since antiquity. Any kingdom or empire that has controlled the Gallipoli peninsula has also mastered the flow of trade across both Europe and Asia.

# The Waterways of Turkey

Europe is separated from Asia by two straits and a small sea. The first strait is the Dardanelles, sometimes referred to by its ancient Greek name Hellespont. Because the other strait, the Bosporus, is very narrow, it has, in the twentieth century, been spanned by two suspension bridges. The Bosporus Bridge was opened in 1973 and carries traffic between Thrace and Anatolia.

Interestingly, because Turkey is surrounded by several different seas, its coasts experience wide

Formed 10,000 years ago, the Black Sea stretches 720 miles (1,159 kilometers) and has a depth of 7,257 feet (2,212 meters). This view of the Black Sea is from the coast of Turkey, which is one of the six countries that border it.

Agri Dagi (Mount Ararat),
means "Mountain of Pain" in
Turkish. According to the biblical story of Genesis, Noah's
ark landed on Mount Ararat
more than 4,300 years ago.

variations in saline levels. For example, the Black Sea has a salinity of eighteen parts per thousand, while the Mediterranean Sea has a salinity of thirty-eight parts per thousand. This variation in salt levels means that Turkey supports many different ecosystems along its coastlines, since most plants and animals can tolerate only a limited range in salinity. As a result, the same kinds of plants and animals that live along the coast of the Black Sea could not survive along the coasts of the Mediterranean or the Aegean.

Two great rivers that gave rise to important and successful civilizations have sources in Turkey: the Tigris and the Euphrates. In the Middle East, for example, many cultures rose and fell along the banks of the Tigris and Euphrates Rivers, including the Sumerians, the Akkadians, the Assyrians, and the Babylonians. In Turkey, the Tigris is called the Dicle, and the Euphrates is the Firat. Modern Turkey has engineered the rivers' power with sophisticated dams that provide electricity to several Turkish cities.

This tobacco field in Turkey is one of many found along the coast of the Black Sea. Currently, Turkey ranks fifth in the world for total tobacco production. On average, Turkey exports 100,000 tons (101,605 metric tons) of tobacco per year.

Turkey has seven river basins. Those that empty into the Black Sea are the Sakarya, Kizilirmak Yesilirmak, and Coruh. A few smaller rivers that also empty into the Black Sea are the Ikizdere, Hursit Cayi, and Firtina. This region has the highest waterfall in Turkey, along the Totum River.

The Kocacay River flows into the Sea of Marmara, while the Kücük Menderes and Gediz Rivers flow into the Aegean. This area is also home to the Büyük Menderes River, which in ancient times was named the Maeander. Because the river's course was very twisty, eventually the name of the river became synonymous with anything that did not travel in a straight line. In English, we still use the word "meander" to describe someone or something that travels in a roundabout manner.

Several rivers, especially those that attract tourists, flow into the Mediterranean Sea. They include the Aksu, Koprucay, Manavgat, Goksu, Ceyhan, and Seyhan. The waterfalls on these rivers attract visitors because of their beauty.

Two rivers, the Aras and the Kura, flow into the Caspian Sea, which is really a large inland lake located outside Turkey's borders. Turkey has two large inland lakes of its own, the Tuz Gölü and Van Gölü, or Lake Van. Because these lakes do not drain into the ocean, they remain salty. The minerals brought into the basins by the rivers cannot drain the salt away. In fact, Tuz Gölü means "salt lake" in Turkish.

## Climate

Turkey's climate is varied because it is home to different geographies. Its coasts, mountains, and plateaus offer Turks a wide range of temperatures from mild summers to freezing winters. The west coast region, often host to tourists year-round, has the most consistent temperatures and is usually around 68° Fahrenheit (20° Celsius). The southern coast even has palm trees, which require tropical temperatures to survive. In general, the coasts receive a great deal of rain. The Central Plateau, surrounded as it is by mountains, is much drier and colder. This region of Turkey may only receive about fourteen inches of rain annually, while the coasts get at least twice that amount. Winters in the mountains, of course, are very cold, dipping to frigid temperatures and receiving annual snowfalls. Because of its varied climate, Turkey is also home to many of the world's cultivated plants such as cherries, apricots, almonds, figs, hazelnuts, lentils, and chickpeas. The fig species *F. caria* is named for an area of southern Turkey. And the cherry's scientific name, *Cerasus*, comes from the name of a province on the shores of the Black Sea. Today, this area is called Giresun.

## Flora and Fauna

More than thirty wild species of wheat currently grow in Turkey. Plant conservation is especially important because most of the world's cultivated wheat crops are genetically similar—or even identical—to each other. If a disease were to wipe out most of the world's wheat, the wild wheat of Turkey would become an agricultural gold mine. Turkey—like Mexico, Peru, and China—is designated as one of the world's most important centers for cultivated plants, a determination made by the International Union for the Conservation of Nature, the World Wildlife Fund, and the International Plant Genetic Resource Institute.

Approximately 80,000 Turkish peasants grow poppy flowers on small, privately owned farms. Peasants harvest these plants in the fall and use the money to supplement their income between seasons.

An aerial view of the western Turkish town of Duzce shows the destruction caused by a 7.2 magnitude earthquake on November 12, 1999. The earthquake killed 320 people, wounded 1,000 more, and destroyed at least 300 buildings. Approximately three months earlier, a 7.4 magnitude quake rocked the Turkish city of Izmit, killing thousands and causing billions of dollars' worth of damage.

Turkey also grows many foreign crops that have been imported to the region over the millennia. These include citrus fruits, tobacco, olives, cotton, rice, barley, and beets.

Although humans have lived in Turkey for thousands of years, the country has large tracts of undeveloped land. Along the Mediterranean coast, one can find undisturbed pine trees, oaks, and junipers. Myrtle and laurel trees also grow along the coast of the Black Sea. The mountainsides abound with oaks, beeches, and elms. Much of the Central Plateau is grassland.

In ancient times, one might have commonly run across bears, wolves, or elephants while traveling in Asia Minor. The lion gates at Hattusas, for example, show that the Hittites were familiar with these large felines. However, lions, bears, wolves, and elephants are no longer in this region. Other animals have fared better over the centuries, despite increasing human populations. Deer, pheasants, and sheep continue to be plentiful. A few leopards still survive in the most remote areas of the mountains, but their population is also dwindling.

Other endangered animals that call Turkey home are monk seals, loggerhead turtles, and the pygmy cormorant. Today, Turkey's Ministry of the Environment oversees programs that aid these animals' survival. The monk seals, which are no longer found in the western Mediterranean area, are flourishing along the Turkish coast. They can be seen in the Sea of Marmara or the Black Sea, but they are most plentiful on the Aegean coast, especially around the city of Izmir. Interestingly, the name of the city comes from an ancient Phoenician word for seal.

Although tourism is important to the nation, it has not been allowed to overtake Turkey's landscape. Recently, development plans were canceled in Koycegiz to preserve turtle breeding grounds, an area later declared environmentally protected. Today, the Turtle Preservation Committee safeguards nearly twenty Turkish beaches.

# Ankara

The capital of Turkey is Ankara, which was chosen over Istanbul to be the capital by Atatürk in the 1920s. He felt that a city in the Central Plateau reflected a revitalized Turkey more so than the old capital of Istanbul. Ankara currently has a population of almost 3 million people. This makes it much smaller than Istanbul, which is home to more than 10 million residents.

Ankara is Turkey's fourth capital since the foundation of the Ottoman Empire. Before Istanbul, the capital cities were at Bursa in Anatolia and Edirne in Thrace. Edirne, called Adrianople in ancient times, was named for the Roman emperor Hadrian.

Istanbul itself, with its large and growing population, is divided into different sections. The Anatolian part is called Uskudar. The Golden Horn, an inlet that has its source in the Bosporus Strait, divides the larger section of the city located in Thrace into northern and southern sections. The southern section is where one can find great architectural wonders like the Hagia Sophia, the Blue Mosque, Topkapi Palace, and the Süleymaniye Mosque.

Today, many resort cities are becoming well-known vacation destinations for tourists. Izmir, which was called Smyrna in ancient times, is on the Aegean coast. Roman and Greek ruins, the chance to glimpse endangered monk seals, and the beaches draw people from around the world. The city of Alanya, often referred to as the Turkish Riviera, is a tourist hot spot on the Mediterranean coast known for its beaches and rocky hills.

Turkey has such a wide range of climates, plants, and animals that one would have to travel the entire country to see its true range of environments and ecosystems.

This view of Ankara, Turkey's capital since 1923, is from the Ankara Citadel, a historical symbol for the city. Galatians laid the citadel's original groundwork in 278 BC. The Romans completed the structure after the Galatians became part of the Roman Empire.

وَعارَض وهو في يده اليسرى وَغز على وسط خط الميدان حتى يصلوا الى وسط الموكب

ثم يتناول العنان مع الدرقة بشماله ويضرب بقائم السيف قبة الدرقة ويثنى عليها

بالدرابة ويرد فرسه يمينا ويدرق بالدرقة يسارا عن كهل الوزير ويرجع على خط الوارس

الكبير ويحيى خلفه يفعل كفعل الاول ويرد فرسه شمالا على خط الوارس الكبير

ويحيى الثالث يفعل كفعل صاحبه ويرد فرسه يمينا ويحيى الاول فيفعل كل فعل الاول والاورد

# THE PEOPLE

## 2

## The Ancient Hittites and the Modern Turks

**P**eople have been living in the area that is now Turkey for thousands of years. Archaeologists discovered that they lived in organized settlements, and possibly even under kings, during the early centuries of the Bronze Age. Many of these settlements are between the Kizil Irmak (Red River) and the southern shore of the Black Sea. Like the Egyptians, these people excavated shaft tombs for their rulers.

Scholars refer to these people as Hittites. Today, no one is certain what language Hittites spoke or where they originated. The main Hittite site is called Çatal Höyük.

Sometime during the early Bronze Age, however, perhaps around 2300 BC, several waves of Indo-Europeans migrated into the area now known as Turkey. These were the Luwians, the Palaians, and the Nesites. Because they spoke an Indo-European language, scholars speculate that they originated northeast of Anatolia, perhaps in what is now Russia. Within several centuries, the dominant city of the area was Nesa. The city's prominence led to Nesite becoming the main commercial language of Anatolia.

## The Hittites

By the late Bronze Age, a Hittite Empire (1700–1200 BC) had formed with its capital at Hattusas, 90 miles (150 kilometers) east of modern-day Ankara. Excavations

This Arabic illumination of mamluks on horseback *(left)* dates from the fifteenth century. Double walls called the Lion's Gate *(above)* surround the Hittite city of Hattusas. This historic landmark is a World Heritage Site because of the construction of its temples, royal residences, and fortifications, as well as its beautiful ornamentation.

This relief of a Hittite noble dates from the eighth century BC. Archaeologists discovered it in 1947 while excavating a frontier fort of the late Hittite people in Karatepe, Turkey.

of Hattusas suggest that the ancient city was massive. Archaeologists and scholars have also discovered that the Hittites kept detailed written records, maintained a large army, and were especially talented artisans who were among the first people to work with iron.

The native Hittite culture had mixed with the immigrant Indo-European civilizations and gave rise to a people who used Nesite as their court language. Still, the people kept their names from the Hittite language, including the name of their kingdom, the Land of Hatti.

The Nesite language was used not only in court but in all government documents as well. Though it might not have been the language of the common people, all government administrators and scribes would have understood it. In a land where many languages were spoken, Nesite united the Hittite people.

Scholars believe the first king of the Hittites was Labarna, who reigned around the middle of the seventeenth century BC. Though he most likely ruled over a small area at first, he soon engaged in military campaigns to conquer surrounding lands. Legends tell us that this was the period during which the Trojan War was supposed to have taken place.

## Troy

In Hittite records, it is clear that a vassal city called Wilusa was situated northwest of Anatolia in the area where the Greeks claimed Troy—or Truva in Turkish—was located. The site is located in the area now referred to as Troy, or Hissarlik-Troy,

German archaeologist Heinrich Schliemann (1822–1890), the man who located the ancient city of Troy, used the work of Homer and local historians to excavate supposed Troy cities throughout Turkey. This full-page sketching, which appeared in *Harper's Weekly* on January 23, 1873, shows Schliemann's excavation sites.

DR. SCHLIEMANN'S EXCAVATIONS AT HISSARLIK—FROM THE EAST.

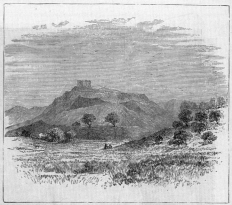

DR. SCHLIEMANN'S EXCAVATIONS AT HISSARLIK—FROM THE WEST.

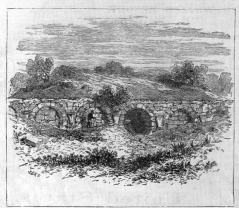

REMAINS OF A THEATRE, ALEXANDRIA TROAS.

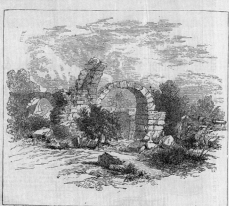

REMAINS OF A PALACE, ALEXANDRIA TROAS.

TEMPLE OF MINERVA, CAPE COLONNA, SCENE OF FALCONER'S "SHIPWRECK."

KALAMITZA BAY, ISLAND OF SKYROS.

## ANCIENT TROY.

WHETHER DR. SCHLIEMANN has unearthed the remains of Priam's Troy, in his excavations at Hissarlik, or those of some still more ancient city, there is no question as to the interest and importance of his discoveries. The excavations, which are very extensive, reveal the remains of walls of wide circuit, and a great quantity of pottery has been brought to light. Some of the earthen jars found many feet beneath the surface are of great size, capable of containing from forty to fifty gallons each. The remains indicate that the place had been destroyed by fire. About thirty feet below the surface the remains of a sloping pavement, evidently the entrance to some gateway, have been uncovered, and are in a very fair state of preservation. The slabs of which it is made are not very large, and appear to be formed of a kind of composition. A great portion of the walls appears to be formed of mud. In parts they are composed of regular stones near the surface, and of irregular ones deeper down.

In connection with the sketch of Hissarlik we give several views of other interesting spots in the Greek Archipelago and the Troad. Alexandria Troas, lying about nine miles south of the Plain of Troy, has been for centuries the magazine whence the Turks have drawn the stone balls which they fire from the batteries about Constantinople. The site is covered with a beautiful forest of dwarf oak. The lines of ancient walls are still quite traceable. The remains of the theatre, stadium, palace, and gateway are in the best preservation. The ruins of the palace especially are most interesting.

Cape Colonna, the ancient Sunium, which forms the limit of the Gulf of Ægina, exhibits on its summit the ruins of the Temple of Minerva. Of this spot Lord BYRON has said : "In all Attica, if we except Athens itself and Marathon, there is no scene more interesting than Cape Colonna. To the antiquary and artist, sixteen columns are an inexhaustible source of observation and design ; to the philosopher, the supposed scene of many of PLATO's conversations will not be unwelcome ; and the traveler will be struck with the beauty of the prospect over 'Isles that crown the Ægean deep ;' " but Colonna has yet an additional interest to students of English poetry as the actual spot of FALCONER's Shipwreck, a poem that deserves to be better known to readers of the present day.

Kalamitza Bay, in the island of Skyros, possesses many attractions. On this island Thetis concealed her son Achilles in woman's attire among the daughters of Lycomedes, in the vain hope of saving him from the fate which awaited him before the walls of Troy. Here also Pyrrhus, the son of Achilles, was brought up, and was taken by Ulysses to the Trojan war. Skyros was once celebrated for its quarries of variegated marble, of which no traces remain.

Displayed at the Archaeological Museum in Istanbul, this tablet is the world's earliest surviving peace treaty, created between the Egyptians and Hittites in 1269 BC.

and was excavated by Heinrich Schliemann in AD 1871–1872. Over a century of excavations, nine levels of the ancient city have been uncovered, each representing a separate period from about 3600 to 100 BC. Overall, scholars have discovered that this city had a strong trade relationship with the Mycenean Greeks. There are many reasons the Greeks may have launched assaults there—fishing rights or trade wars, for example—but these were likely small incidents that took place intermittently over decades.

Archaeologists and historians believe that they encountered the Troy of legend at the seventh layer of excavation, a site often referred to as Troy VII. At that time, the city had large towers and thick walls; it was an imposing edifice. This discovery indicates the city was wealthy enough to build such defenses and to maintain them.

However, the walls of this level are cracked. Some people think this was because of the so-called Trojan War, while others say an earthquake could have caused the damage. Even if an earthquake caused the walls to crack, no one can be certain whether the damage happened during ancient times or more recently.

Most likely, the city of Wilusa had occasional troubles with its Greek trading partners, and these small-scale wars were later combined into one large

The fifth-century Greek vase painting depicts the Battle of Troy. The art of the ancient Greeks is referred to as classical art, and the best examples of this work are often found on vases, which have largely been preserved in tombs.

war for poetic and storytelling purposes. In that sense, the Trojan War actually happened, though Greek writers most likely embellished the facts centuries later, such as in Homer's poetic epics *The Iliad* and *The Odyssey*.

The last king of the Hittites was Suppiluliuma II, who was crowned in 1207 BC. At this time, new migrations of people, a weakened central government, and possibly earthquakes were more hurdles than the king could overcome. The reign of the Hittites was over.

## The Lydians, the Greeks, and the Persians

By 715 BC, the Assyrians had taken advantage of the lack of central authority and had spread their empire into parts of Anatolia. But the Assyrian Empire collapsed only a century later. In place of Assyrian authority, local kings began dominating small areas of their own.

It was in one of these kingdoms, known as Lydia, on the western coast of Anatolia, that people first began minting coins. The crude coins were made of a naturally occurring mixture of gold and silver called electrum. Nuggets of this metal could be found in the River

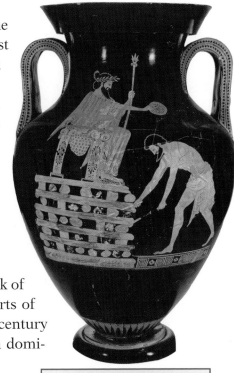

Located in the Louvre Museum in Paris, France, this Greek vase by Myson dates from between 500 and 490 BC and depicts King Croesus of Lydia on his funeral pyre.

Pactolus, which ran through the Lydian city of Sardis. Within a century of the first minted coins, around 560 BC, the Lydians had perfected the technique of separating silver from gold. The Lydian king, Croesus, issued the world's first coinage in the two metals. The kingdom was so rich with gold and silver that even today, someone who is very wealthy is sometimes described as being as "rich as Croesus."

King Croesus was defeated in 546 BC by Persian armies, and Persians became the new overlords of Anatolia. The area remained under their control until Alexander the Great defeated the Persians in 334 BC. Alexander's influence extended over much of the known world of the time. Alexander died young, probably of malaria, however, and Anatolia was soon thrown into economic and political turmoil. This chaos continued for most of the next two centuries until the coming of the Romans around 133 BC.

This statue of Constantine I is located in York, England, where he was proclaimed emperor of the western Roman provinces in AD 306. By 324, Constantine founded the Byzantine Empire, moved the capital of Rome to Byzantium on the site of the ancient Greek port, and renamed it Constantinople in AD 330.

# The Byzantine Empire

Roman rule brought peace and economic prosperity to the region now known as Turkey, and Christianity became the main religion. The area became so important that in AD 324 the Roman emperor Constantine I moved his capital to the old Greek city of Byzantium, which was later renamed Constantinople—present-day Istanbul.

In the west, Rome fell to barbarians, Goths who invaded the region in AD 476. But in the east, Constantinople remained intact for another thousand years. This is known as the time of the Byzantine Empire.

The Byzantine Empire, though Latin in origin, quickly became Greek in culture and language. Over the centuries, the Byzantine emperors fought off attacks by Arabs, Slavs, and Persians. But the empire was weakened, especially after the Venetians

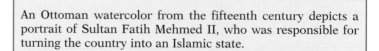

An Ottoman watercolor from the fifteenth century depicts a portrait of Sultan Fatih Mehmed II, who was responsible for turning the country into an Islamic state.

This painting, circa 1537, is located in the Monastery of Moldovita, Romania. It depicts the siege of Constantinople in 1453 by Turkish Muslims. The Christian inhabitants of the city paraded sacred icons, asking God for help in the conflict.

organized the Fourth Crusade in 1204 and conquered the city to take the riches of the empire back to Venice. The Crusades had begun when Christians went to war against Muslims in the Middle East, but in the Fourth Crusade, both sides were Christian. Today, Turkey's Roman ruins attract thousands of tourists every year. In fact, Turkey houses the second-largest collection of Roman ruins—including the largest Roman amphitheater—in the world.

## The Ottoman Empire

The Seljuk Turks captured much of Anatolia from the Byzantine Empire while it was weakened, but they were never able to capture Constantinople. It was not until the Ottoman Turks moved into the area that Constantinople became seriously threatened. The Ottoman Turks, under Orhan I, gained their first foothold in

Housed at the Biblioteca Nacional in Madrid, Spain, this twelfth-century version of John Skylitzes' manuscript *Synopsis Historiarum* is the only surviving illuminated chronicle in Greek. Within it are 574 illustrations depicting Byzantine life, including this cavalry battle between the Byzantines and the Seljuks.

This copper engraving of Janissaries and Spahis by artist A. Mallet dates from between 1683 and 1686. In the Ottoman Empire, Janissaries consisted of war captives who gradually gained power in the empire. In 1826, Sultan Mahmud II (1808–1839) had the Janissaries massacred by his loyal cavalry, the Spahis.

Thrace at Gallipoli in 1345. The Turks largely took control of the Balkans, conquering parts of present-day Serbia, Romania, and Bulgaria. Although the Ottoman Empire surrounded Constantinople, it remained unconquered for the next century.

In 1453, Sultan Mehmed II (1451–1481), called the Conqueror, finally put an effort into overtaking Constantinople. By this time, cannons were used in warfare, even though they were often defective and difficult to maintain. Mehmed II had several cast and dragged to locations overlooking the walls of the city. After months of bombardment, the city was weakened. The Turks got over the walls and overtook the region.

From that point on, Constantinople was known as Istanbul, which is from the Greek phrase *eis tan polin*, or "to the city." One of the first things Mehmed II did after taking the city was to order that the Christian church of Hagia Sophia be converted into an Islamic mosque. What had been the center of a Christian empire was now the capital of a Muslim one.

During the Ottoman Empire, the sultan and his family lived in Topkapi Palace, a sprawling building that could house hundreds of people. Other building projects, such as the Süleymaniye Mosque, helped to transform Istanbul's skyline into a forest of minarets.

## The Janissaries

The army of the Ottomans was largely made up of feudal levies, peasants conscripted to fight for the sultan. But soon the sultan found another way to form an

Titled "Tightening the Grip," this 1877 political cartoon by Sir John Tenniel accompanied a poem encouraging England to denounce the Turkish massacre of Bulgarian Christians and to ally with Russia in the Turkish-Russian War.

army: levy children from conquered people. This levy, or demand, known in Turkish as *devflirme*, was composed of young boys taken from Christian families. The boys made up a military group called the Janissaries.

Far from being dreaded, the levy was welcomed by many families. Though the children would be raised Muslim, they would be educated, fed, and protected. Some would die in battle, of course, but the life of a Janissary was a rich and stable one, compared with the lives of the boys' families in many of the Balkan villages of the time.

The Janissary corps of the Ottoman army were the terror of Europe for several centuries. Janissaries were zealous converts to their new religion and fanatically faithful to the sultan. However, over time, their devotion waned. The status associated with being a Janissary—despite the fact that Janissaries were slaves—was so great that elite families petitioned the sultan to allow their sons to fight. By the year 1700, the devflirme was discontinued, since it was no longer necessary to conscript boys.

This change signaled a change in the Janissaries as well. Rather than being fanatically faithful slave-soldiers, they were now wealthy men of noble families. The sultan became less the overlord of the Janissaries and more their prisoner. The first sultan to challenge them was killed in 1622, and it wasn't until two centuries later, in 1826, that Mahmud II slaughtered the Janissaries during a parade. The power of the elite corps of the army was finally broken.

Prime Minister Ramsay MacDonald of Great Britain (seated at small table) signs the Lausanne Treaty on July 24, 1923. Imposed by the Allied powers on Turkey after World War I, this treaty nearly devastated the country as a national state.

## The Fall of the Ottoman Empire

One of the problems plaguing the empire was the matter of succession. Only one son could become sultan, but because the sultans had many wives and concubines, they often had a surplus of sons. In the early kingdoms, sons were sent to far provinces to learn how to rule. However, once one son secured the throne, he was expected to kill his brothers before they could threaten his new position as sultan, thus preventing a potential civil war.

Later sultans did not kill their brothers, but kept them locked in their own quarters near the harem. These quarters, known as *kafes*, or cages, were where many male children of the sultans spent their entire lives after leaving their mothers' care.

Mustafa Kemal—known as Atatürk, or Father of the Turks—and his entourage travel through the streets of Anatolia. Under Atatürk's leadership, Turkey was the first Muslim nation to become a republic.

## The Kurds

The Kurdish people, spread across several Middle Eastern countries such as Turkey, Iraq, and Iran, have struggled for years to gain independence. These people continue to fight for their autonomy based on agreements that were put into effect after World War I and that promised Kurds their own  homeland, Kurdistan. Throughout their history of fighting for independence, the Kurds have faced many casualties, such as in 1988, when thousands fled to Turkey from Iraq to escape attack by deadly chemicals. In Turkey, the Kurdish Workers' Party (PKK) finally discontinued this fight in 1999, after launching a guerrilla war in pursuit of its claim for a separate land for more than fifteen years. The conflicts claimed about 36,500 lives.

Each system was flawed. In the first system, a sultan could kill off his brothers, but if he had no son, the succession was in danger upon his death. In the second system, the sultan's brothers remained alive and could become sultan, but they were not prepared for life outside their cages. Such a man had never been outside the palace, let alone given orders. Sultans who had been prisoners their entire lives tended to be mentally unstable, or at least became very bad rulers.

## The Republic of Turkey

By the early twentieth century, the Ottoman Empire was crumbling. Viewed by the West as uncivilized, the Ottomans were isolated and in jeopardy. A group called

On July 22, 1974, Turkish air force pilots drop supplies to Turkish ground troops in Cyprus, Greece. Turkey claimed that it invaded Cyprus in order to protect the 18 percent minority of Turks living on the island.

the Young Turk Committee gained enough power to frighten the sultan into calling parliamentary elections for the first time. In 1923, after World War I, the Treaty of Lausanne outlined the borders of modern Turkey and the Republic of Turkey was born. Mustafa Kemal, who was soon to take the name Atatürk ("Father of the Turks"), became its first president.

## The Reforms of Kemal Atatürk

Atatürk, who was president of Turkey from 1923 to 1938, instituted many reforms in Turkey that modernized and, in some aspects, westernized the nation. His hope was to make Turkey a secular state, and not one that he believed was too firmly entrenched in Islamic tradition. He outlawed the turban and fez, the tall cap men traditionally wore. Atatürk did not make

This Kurdish woman displays a flag bearing a portrait of Kurdish Workers' Party (PKK) leader Abdullah Ocalan during a demonstration in Strasburg, France, demanding the liberation of the Kurdish rebel leader.

wearing the veil illegal, but discouraged women from covering their faces. Education became available for every boy or girl, no matter how poor. The Latin alphabet was introduced to make the goal of nationwide literacy easier to achieve. Women were given the right to vote in 1930 and to run for public office in 1934. Other changes took place too, such as the adoption of the Gregorian calendar, which replaced the Muslim lunar one. Newer laws that resembled those already in place in the European system also replaced older Islamic law codes.

## Modern Turkey

After Atatürk's death in 1938, Turkey faced many internal problems. Its unstable government was often overtaken by military force. Problems within the country also contributed to civil disturbances, rioting, and street fighting. The oppression of Kurds, a deadly invasion of Cyprus in 1974 that killed an estimated 200,000 people, and several military coups have sometimes threatened the reform movement begun by the Young Turk Committee. Islamic fundamentalist groups also continue to gain power, fortifying underground religious movements and posing a substantial threat to the nation's stability.

Yet Turkey continues to struggle. In fact, in 1993, Tansu Çiller became Turkey's first woman prime minister—a significant achievement for a nation where, only one hundred years ago, women were rarely educated.

# THE TURKISH LANGUAGE

## 3

## From Ancient Greek to Modern Turkish

The Turkish language belongs to a family of languages called Ural-Altaic. More than 150 million people in various countries across eastern Europe and Asia speak Ural-Altaic languages. The Uralic half of the family contains languages like Finnish and Hungarian while the Altaic half contains languages like Turkish.

All Ural-Altaic languages share two important features, which are agglutination and vowel harmony. Agglutination means that multiple suffixes are added to a root word to indicate number and gender. Vowel harmony means that the vowels used in the suffixes agree with the vowel in the root word. For example, "house" is *ev*. "At the house" is *evde*. But for the word "table," which is *masa*, "at the table" becomes *masada*.

Turkish has no articles; that is, no words like "a," "an," or "the." The standard word order of a Turkish sentence is subject-object-verb. This differs from English, which generally has the verb following the subject.

At least sixty million people speak Turkish, which is the official language of Turkey. There are also native speakers of Turkish in Bulgaria, Macedonia, Greece, Uzbekistan, Kazakhstan, Kyrgyzstan, Tajikistan, and Azerbaijan. Nineteen percent of the population of Cyprus speaks Turkish, which is the co-official language alongside Greek.

Because of immigration, more than one million Turkish speakers live in Germany and other northern European countries, and roughly 25,000 live in the United States.

During the reign of Sultan Süleyman from 1520 to 1566, an illustrated book about the Ottoman leader introduced a new artistic form in the country called Saz, seen in this image *(left)* entitled *Sultan Süleyman the Magnificent Hunting in Western Anatolia*. Saz-style decoration was developed by Sahkuli, a court-appointed artist who hailed from Baghdad. The English translation of the white Koranic inscription *(above)* reads, "In the name of God, the compassionate and holy one."

A column, found in the north Aegean Sea at the ruins of Troy, is inscribed in Greek. Archaeologists have uncovered the remains of what they believe to be Troy in Ilium, Turkey.

Turkish is taught at many universities in the United States, including Cornell University and the University of Illinois. Within Turkey itself, the Turk Dil Kurumu Turkish Language Academy functions as an organization that establishes linguistic standards.

Although Turkish is divided into western and eastern dialects, it is the eastern Anatolian dialect spoken around Istanbul that is used for standard Turkish. All Turkish dialects are mutually intelligible; that is, someone who speaks the western Danubian dialect would easily understand someone speaking the eastern Karamanli dialect. This similarity between different dialects indicates that they have not been separated from the parent Turkish language for very long.

## Adopted Words

Turkish entered the region with the Ottoman Turks. Because the founder of the

Dating from AD 1250, this scene by Abd al Mu'min al Khayyam accompanies the poem "The Romance of Varqa and Gulshah" and was written by Urwa. This manuscript, located in the Topkapi Palace Museum in Istanbul, is the only illustrated version of the verses.

Turkish chieftain Osman Gazi (1258–1326), founder of the Ottoman Empire, is shown seated during a meeting with a Byzantine governor. In 1293, Osman emerged as a leader in the Turkish conquest against the Byzantine Empire.

Ottoman dynasty was named Osman Gazi, Turkish is also sometimes called Osmanli. Since the Ottoman Turks had converted to Islam and had passed through India and Persia on their migrations, many Persian and Arabic words had been added to the language. For instance, the Turkish phrase for "hello," *merhaba*, would also be used in present-day Iran or in African countries like Egypt or Morocco.

Turkish has adopted words from other languages, such as English. *Milyon* ("million"), *trafik* ("traffic"), *tren* ("train"), *bankanyn* ("bank"), *otel* ("hotel"), and *telefon* ("telephone") have all been taken from English.

But the flow of words goes both ways. English has adopted several Turkish words, too, such as yogurt, pastrami, pilaf, and baklava.

The original Turkish form of "pastrami" is *pastyrma*. A "pastyrma summer" refers to the last hot days of summer when cured meats were traditionally dried in the open air. In English, we

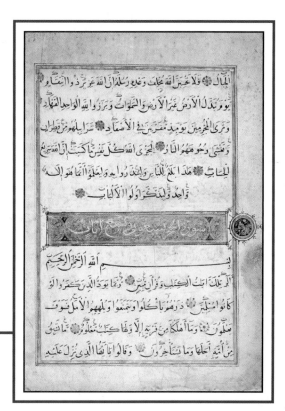

Housed in the Pierpont Morgan Library in New York, this folio of the Koran, dating back as early as the fourteenth century, is an example of the Arabic writing that once dominated the language of Turkey. Like all versions of the Koran, this manuscript contains only text, since Muslims respect the religious principles of Uthman, the third caliph of Islam, who forbade the representation of Allah or Muhammad.

use the phrase "Indian summer" to mean this time of warm, hazy weather that occurs in October or November. In the story, "In the Park by the Pier" by modern Turkish author Füruzan, a character says, "This may be a pastyrma summer lasting until the end of November . . . this is Istanbul, you can never tell."

Over the centuries when the Ottoman Empire reigned, Turkish was written in the Arabic script, which was not suited for the sounds of the Turkish language. Court documents were often drafted in Persian, as was the court poetry of the time. More and more non-Turkish words were incorporated into the language. The language spoken in the Ottoman court, which had originally been the same as the language of commoners, began to diverge from the spoken tongue of most of the population. The Turkish spoken by average citizens had far fewer borrowed words, but it was considered the language of the uneducated masses. Over time, the court language took on an increased Persian flavor.

## Modern Turkish

That Persian influence decreased in the 1920s. Turkish was declared the official

## Turkish Words

| | |
|---|---|
| good morning | günaydyn |
| excuse me | afedersiniz |
| yes/no | evet/hayyr |
| please | lütfen |
| thank you | tepekkür ederim |
| good-bye | hopçakal |
| happy birthday | iyi ki doddun |
| child | çocuk |

## Turkish Pronunciation Key

Turkish has several letters that either do not occur in English or are pronounced differently than they are in English.

| | | |
|---|---|---|
| **c** | = | *j* as in jam |
| **ç** | = | *ch* as in church |
| **d** | = | is usually silent, but between vowels can be pronounced like a soft *y* |
| **j** | = | *zh* as the "s" in pleasure or measure |
| **p** | = | *sh* as in ship |
| **ö** | = | like the "ur" in fur |
| **ü** | = | like the "ew" in few |
| **y** | = | like "ir" in shirt |

This illustration, entitled *Sultan Süleyman at the Battle of Mohac*, from the 1588 manuscript *The Military Campaigns of Süleyman* is by Sah Kulu, who painted the history of the sultan in a style influenced by the East.

Turkish books for sale in a book bazaar. Turkish is an ancient language with a history that stretches back more than 6,000 years. Today, approximately 65 million people speak Turkish throughout Europe and Asia.

language of the country, and steps were taken to remove Persian and Arabic words from the language, replacing them with Turkish equivalents. A version of the Roman alphabet, with a few special characters added to better reflect the sounds of Turkish, was designed. Everyone in the country was forced to convert to the new alphabet. Most people could not read the Arabic script anyway, except for scholars and government and military workers.

Armies of people were trained in the new alphabet and sent out to the country-side to teach everyone to read and write in Turkish. Because of this massive campaign, literacy rates in Turkey have risen from perhaps 10 percent at the beginning of the twentieth century to more than 80 percent at the beginning of the twenty-first century.

An immense effort was also put forth into rooting out borrowed words in standard Turkish. But over the decades, Turkish has increased its core vocabulary. Borrowed words have largely disappeared.

With the change in alphabet and core vocabulary, Turkish eventually became more popular as the language of

In the Old Jewish Quarter of Balat, a section in Istanbul, this Muslim vendor sells produce. Nearly 27,000 Jews live in Turkey, of which 24,500 live in the city of Istanbul.

Turkish literature. Previously, most poetry was written in Persian. In the twentieth century, however, the emphasis has been on using the native language in new ways. Authors have expanded literature to include Japanese-style haiku poetry and stream-of-consciousness novels. Others have written Turkish mystery stories and science fiction. Turkish, which was for centuries overlaid with a Persian and Arabic patina, has been resurrected as a vibrant, expressive language of its own.

Although Turkish is the official language of Turkey, other languages are also spoken there. One of these is Kurdish, which is spoken by about 11 million people in Turkey. Kurdish, unlike Turkish, is an Indo-European language like English. It is closely related to Persian.

In this photograph, Mustafa Kemal—known as Atatürk—is seen teaching the Turkish alphabet. Many of Atatürk's reforms began with education. He is quoted as saying, "The government's most creative and significant duty is education." Under his leadership, the literacy rate rose from less than 9 percent in 1923 when the Republic of Turkey was founded to more than 33 percent by 1938.

# TURKISH MYTHS AND LEGENDS

## 4

Many well-known myths and legends take place in Turkey, including some that are thousands of years old. Some of these tales originated from the period before the region known as Turkey was settled. These ancient stories, some stemming from nomads traveling eastward from Asia, were passed down from generation to generation. Other tales may sound more familiar to Westerners, such as those that are derived from the ancient Greeks.

## Greek Mythology

In one myth, the king of the Greek gods, Zeus, liked a beautiful woman named Io. But his wife, Hera, found out about Zeus's interest. To protect Io from Hera, Zeus turned Io into a cow. But Hera wasn't tricked and she sent flies to torment the cow, who swam across the strait of water separating Europe from Asia. The strait has been known as the Ford of the Cow—the Bosporus—ever since.

In another Greek myth, a queen named Nephele feared that her children's lives were in danger. She placed them on the back of a golden ram, who was charged with bringing them to safety. The daughter, Helle, fell off the ram into a strait of water that separates Europe from Asia, which was named the Hellespont in her honor. Today, that stretch of water is called the Dardanelles. The ram delivered

The colossal sculpture of the head of Antiochus I *(left)* atop Mount Nemrut was once part of an ancient spiritual site. Antiochus I of Kommage built the shrine as a funerary sanctuary dedicated to his Greco-Roman ancestors. Along with the military leader are sculptures of the heads of such gods as Apollo, Zeus, Hermes, and Hercules. Dating from the mid-nineteenth century, this image *(above)* shows a man recounting a story from *The Arabian Nights* to a crowd in Pergamum, Turkey.

the son to the kingdom of Colchis, where it was sacrificed to the gods and its fleece was kept in a sacred grove. Colchis was located on the northern coast of Anatolia, which today is Turkey.

## Jason and the Golden Fleece

Years later, Jason, a hero of Greek mythology, undertook a voyage to retrieve the Golden Fleece of the ram and return it to Greece. He had a ship built, the *Argo*, and gathered a crew of fifty heroes, known as the Argonauts, including Hercules, Theseus, and Orpheus, to go with him on his quest. The ship passed through the Hellespont without incident, but it could not go farther because the next strait was full of rocks that moved by themselves. Certainly any ship that tried to navigate through them would be crushed. The blind prophet Phineas told Jason the trick for passing through the clashing rocks. With the help of his crew and Phineas, Jason succeeded in taking the Golden Fleece from Colchis and returning it to Greece.

## The Trojan War

Even more famous than stories of Io and Jason is the mythical story of the Trojan War. The conflict began with an argument between several Greek goddesses. Hera, Aphrodite, and Athena quarreled over which one of them was the most beautiful. Zeus refused to judge between them and made Paris, the son of the king of Troy, choose. Each goddess tried to bribe Paris with gifts. Finally, Paris chose Aphrodite, who had promised him the most beautiful woman in the world for his wife. Hera and Athena, angry at not being chosen, became Paris's enemies.

Unfortunately, the most beautiful woman in the world, Helen, the queen of the Greek city of Sparta, was already happily married to Menelaus, Sparta's king. She was so beautiful that every man who had sought her hand in marriage had pledged to protect her even if he himself did not become her husband.

Neither Paris nor Aphrodite cared that Helen was married and had so many protectors. Paris took Helen to Troy, while her husband and champions followed behind, prepared to do anything to get her back. The poet Homer described the resulting war and its aftermath in his poems *The Iliad* and *The Odyssey*. The Greeks

This chalk lithograph, colored by R. Weibezahl in 1832, shows Jason from Greek mythology winning the Golden Fleece. According to legend, the fleece was the skin of a golden ram, which hung in a secret grove and was guarded by dragons.

and the Trojans fought for ten years, but finally through trickery—the Greek soldiers hid inside a giant wooden horse to enter Troy—the Greeks succeeded in taking the city. In fact, it was Homer's epic poems that prompted Heinrich Schliemann to search Turkey for the long-ruined city of Troy.

Many famous storytellers came from Anatolia. Aesop, to whom many Greek fables are attributed, may have come from Thrace or the land of Phrygia, which is in present-day Ankara. Homer, the poet who wrote about the Trojan War, may have been born in Izmir and possibly learned the tale about the war from his journeys up and down the Anatolian coast. These storytellers had a feast of cultural riches to choose from, since Anatolia had received stories from both Europe and Asia. Characters like Midas, whose touch could turn objects to gold; Croesus, who owned fabulous wealth; and Gordius, who tied the legendary Gordian knot, were only a few of the subjects of Greek myths with Turkish settings that remain popular to this day.

Published in London, England, in 1892, *Midas' Daughter Turned to Gold* is from Nathaniel Hawthorne's *A Wonder-Book for Girls and Boys*. In the story, Midas, king of Phyrgia, has asked the Greek goddess Dionysus to have whatever he touched turned to gold.

## The Legend of Saint Nicholas

During the first few centuries of the Christian era, many famous elders of the church lived in Anatolia. One of them, who was probably born in the fourth century in the town of Patara, became the bishop of Myra (present-day Demre). Both towns are in Anatolia. This bishop was known for his generous deeds. Over the centuries, his story became so confusing that no one today knows the facts of the story from its legend.

In one tale, a poor man had three daughters who could not marry because they had no money for a dowry. The bishop secretly brought gold into the house of the poor man so that the daughters would be able to find husbands. The poor man found out his benefactor was the bishop and, though the bishop begged him not to tell, told everyone about the gifts.

That bishop was Saint Nicholas. Today, seventeen centuries later, his legend has become so large that people around the world receive presents that are supposed to be from him, either on his feast day of December 6 or on the day of Christ's birth, Christmas. Whether the real Saint Nicholas was generous we'll never know, but the legend of this saint from Turkey has endured.

# Storytelling

The art of Turkish storytelling was infused with Asian and Indian culture when the Turks rode into Asia Minor from central Asia. Their nomadic culture had no written language; stories had to be passed on orally; they were not written down.

Chinese and Indian stories were slowly incorporated into Turkish tales. After conversion to Islam, the Turks adopted stories about the life of the prophet Muhammad. They embraced Persian forms of poetry and the Arabic alphabet, and even used Persian when they eventually started writing.

But the art of the storyteller could not be completely replaced by the written word. Imagine the women of the household listening for the approach of the neighborhood storyteller, for this was one profession that women were allowed to practice. The women of the harem could never allow a man inside, but women were always welcome. Women would gather around to listen as the storyteller began her story.

"Once there was, and once there was not, when the donkey was a town crier and the sieve was in the straw . . ." began many tales. The nonsense beginning was much like the more familiar "Once upon a time . . ." that begins many European stories. The phrase set the tone of the story and prepared listeners for tales of whimsy, heroism, and romance. The standard beginning is called *tekerleme*. The rhythm of the words, as well as their nonsense, propelled the listener out of his or her own world and into the fantasy world of the storyteller.

One tale is about a princess who lived in a crystal kiosk on an island. A kiosk is a house surrounded by a garden. One day, a prince sailed by the kiosk. Although the princess thought he was very handsome, she did not want to reveal herself to him. She disguised herself as a servant and went to meet the prince, who was quite rude. He yelled to his crew, "Up with the sails!" The prince's ship quickly sailed away. The princess then asked her father to build her a ship made of diamonds, which he did. The princess sailed for the prince's city, rented a large house, and waited for the prince. She knew he would be curious to see any woman who sailed a ship made of diamonds and who was wealthy enough to rent the grandest house in the city.

When the prince finally came, he fell in love with her and asked for her hand in marriage. The princess instead went to her sparkling ship and yelled, "Up with the sails," and left the prince behind. Now he knew the identity of this mysterious woman. He sailed again for the crystal kiosk and begged her forgiveness for his rudeness, and the couple were married. Together they lived for many years in great happiness.

In the Karakoy Quarter of Istanbul, Muslim vendors sell tesbeh beads and evil eye protectors. Two historical attractions in this area are the clock tower and Florence Nightingale's room in the Selimiye Barracks, preserved since the Crimean War.

Just as these tales often begin with a standard opening, they usually end with one. The storyteller might end her tale by reciting, "Three apples fell from the sky; the first for me, the second for you, and the third for the one who passes the story on to another."

Repetition is also important in oral story-telling. Repeating phrases engages listeners and helps them to remember the story. Standardized phrases, such as describing a woman to be "as beautiful as a fourteenth of the moon," are expected by listeners. They are delighted to hear these familiar phrases repeated from tale to tale. In these stories, weddings take forty days and forty nights, and characters who travel go "a long way, a short way, through a summer and six months, over hill and dale a straight way."

Though Turkish folktales often mention Islamic traditions like washing and shrouding a body, the tales also retain a pre-Islamic influence and speak of a time before women were confined in harems. Women in Turkish folktales experience as many adventures and have as much courage as men do.

In one tale, an angry sultan gives orders for all women in the region to be killed because his wives have displeased him. "All women are short on brains," he declares. Every woman but one is rounded up and locked in a bathhouse. The last woman is a fierce soldier who has killed giants and gathered great treasure during her adventures. When her husband, a woodcutter, explains this to the sultan, he reverses his order because of his admiration for the heroics of the woodcutter's wife.

## Nasreddin Hoca

Perhaps the most famous storyteller from Turkey was Nasreddin Hoca, a thirteenth-century, quick-witted clown. Everyone in Turkey knows not only his name but most

likely some of his famous sayings as well. His fame has spread beyond Turkey to North Africa, the Middle East, parts of Asia, and the Balkans. He is so famous that many of the stories commonly attributed to him probably never happened but were later invented because of his popularity. Today, scholars do not know if he was one man or several people who were lumped together to create one common folk hero.

Hoca is known as a poet and a person of intelligence, but some of the stories about him describe him as a kind of clown. The trickster or jester character—someone who uses his wits to advance his interests—is common to many cultures. Perhaps Hoca is a combination of an old trickster of legend as well as an actual person.

One story about him claims that he borrowed a cooking pot, and when he returned it, the owner found a smaller pot inside. Hoca told the man that the larger pot gave birth to the smaller pot. The following week, Hoca borrowed the pot yet again, only this time, he did not return it. When the owner wanted to know where his pot was, the poet said that it had died. When the man expressed disbelief, the poet answered, "You are very strange—only last week you had no trouble believing your pot gave birth, and now you won't believe it died!"

Even Hoca's tomb shows his wit. It is hexagonal and sits under a cupola of the same shape. Five of the cupola's walls are open, while the sixth is padlocked. Of course, the lock serves no purpose since the other five sides are accessible. This joke, according to tradition, was Hoca's way of telling people they should smile instead of cry when they visited his tomb.

In modern times, film and television are making the art of storytelling obsolete. Some people, however, are doing what they can to preserve this tradition. The storyteller's tales may survive, but the era of listening to a tale around the fire has since passed.

In July, the International Nasreddin Hoca Festival takes place in Aksehir at the site of Nasreddin's tomb. Stories of Nasreddin Hoca reflect the humor of the Turkish people. This portrait of him dates from 1500.

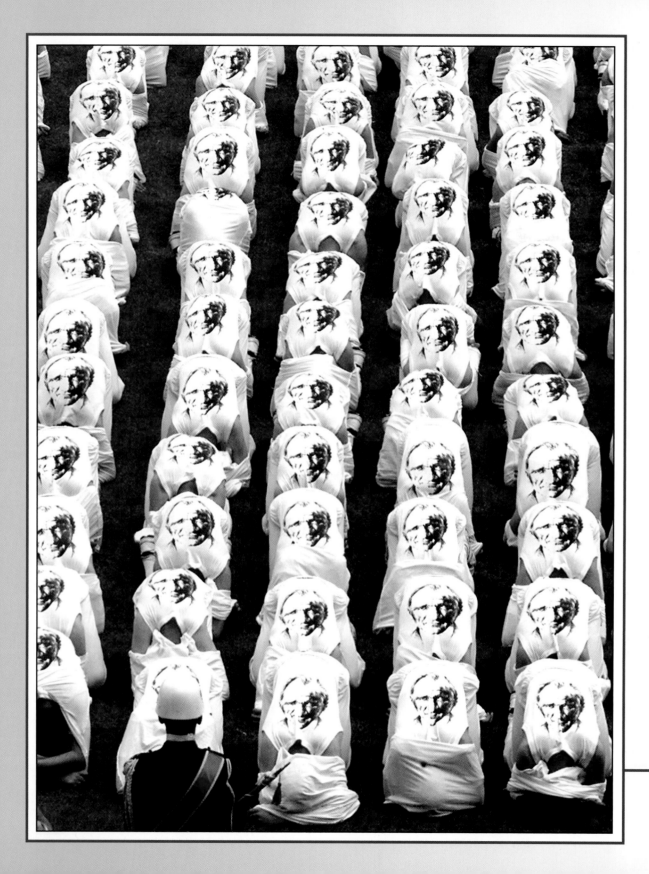

# TURKISH FESTIVALS AND CEREMONIES OF ANTIQUITY AND TODAY

**5**

The Turks celebrate many happy occasions like weddings and births, but they also celebrate different religious festivals during the year. Two of the most important Muslim festivals are the end of Ramadan, known as Ramazan in Turkey, the month-long tradition of Islamic fasting and prayer, and the end of the *hajj*, or pilgrimage to Mecca. During these two separate religious holidays, businesses in Turkey are sometimes closed for several days.

## Seker Bayrami

Ramazan (Ramadan) is the month in which devout Muslims fast during the daylight hours. Many people in Turkey practice Ramazan, but some do not. Because Turkey is a secular state, places like restaurants do not close during this time, although they will have fewer customers than usual.

The typical daylong fast during the month of Ramazan is broken by the *iftar* meal. It is not a large meal, however, because eating a large meal after fasting is not healthy. Instead, a small meal of cheese, sausage, fruit, candy, and salad is perfect after sundown. After the month of Ramazan is over, Turks celebrate the Seker Bayrami, which is a three-day festival. Many sugary sweets are consumed during these three days. Children receive presents, including candy, toys, and new clothing.

The commemoration of Atatürk and Youth and Sports Day are held every year on May 19. On this day, Turks celebrate the Turkish war of independence. In a moment of celebration, military students *(left)* in Kuleli display jerseys with a picture of Atatürk on the back. During Nowruz, a Turkish celebration that marks the arrival of spring, a young boy *(above)* makes the sign for victory as he jumps over a fire.

A Turkish man eats dates in a spice bazaar in Istanbul. Muslims break their fast with dates during Ramadan, the ninth month of the Muslim calendar. Throughout the month, Muslims fast during daylight and eat a small meal in the evening after sundown.

## Apure Bayrami

On the tenth day of the first month of the Muslim calendar, Turks celebrate Apure Bayrami. Two events are commemorated on this day: the death of the prophet Muhammad's grandson Hussein, and the landing of Noah's ark on Mount Ararat.

Tradition says that Noah commanded his wife to make a feast with whatever they had available on the ark. She dutifully combined everything she had left in her larder. The result was a sweet soup with forty ingredients. Today, Turks eat *apure*, a soup made of things like apricots, figs, and walnuts to remember both Hussein and Noah.

People in Turkey also celebrate the birth of the prophet Muhammad. On that day, children are taught some of the prophet's writings and are told stories about his childhood. Colored eggs are often exchanged between friends to celebrate Muhammad's birthday.

The sixteenth-century miniature painting depicts Noah's ark. Many people believe that actual remains of the ark could be preserved in Mount Ararat's ice fields, as it is described in biblical accounts.

Muhammad's birthday is not the only important day of the prophet's life that Turks celebrate. They also celebrate Lele-I-Mirach, the fifth day of the seventh month, upon which Muslims believe the prophet rose to heaven. Mosques are full on this day, a holiday marked more by thoughtfulness rather than by festivity. People are expected to meditate about the prophet, their religion, and their personal beliefs.

## The Feast of the Sacrifice

The most widely observed religious festival in Turkey is Kurban Bayrami, the Feast of the Sacrifice. This festival celebrates the day Abraham was ordered to sacrifice his son, but God provided a ram instead. In Turkey today, every business and family sacrifices a sheep, goat, or even a cow. Even families that are not very religious take part in this festival. Because the animals must be sacrificed a certain way, most families rely on traveling butchers to do the job for them.

When the animal is dead, blood is placed on the foreheads of the family's children for good luck. The family keeps one-third of the meat and gives the rest to the poor. Impoverished families use this annual bounty to survive throughout the year because they can dry and salt the meat to nourish them for many months.

The sheep pictured here will be sacrificed for the Feast of the Sacrifice, or Kurban Bayrami, an important holiday. It is held for three days and remembers the sacrifice Abraham was willing to commit for God.

Very little is wasted during this festival. Even the lungs of the sacrificed animals are traditionally fed to dogs. The animals' wool is donated to organizations for fund-raising. Kurban Bayrami benefits everyone in Turkish society.

## Weddings and Births

Other festivals revolve around Turkish culture. During the days of the Ottoman Empire, for instance, weddings were celebrated for weeks with feasts every day. When one of the daughters of Sultan Mehmet IV was married, more than 50,000 chickens were served for the occasion. The days of such extravagance are gone, but many families still celebrate weddings over the course of several days.

The bride's family hosts the first feast. During the feast, the actual wedding is performed. The following day, the groom's family has a second feast to welcome the bride. These feasts are lavish with many different dishes such as chickpea stew, chicken and rice, and *zerde* (a rice and nut dessert) served to guests. These are normally large events. If the wedding takes place in a small village, for example, everyone in the town will be invited.

After two days of feasting, the bride and groom are fed unsalted chicken for good luck. Afterward, they are allowed to begin their married life together, and their families take leave of their guests by giving them *baklava*, a sweet, nutty pastry.

The details of a Turkish wedding might depend on the section of the country in which a couple is married. In central Turkey, for instance, feasts traditionally have seven courses. In the southeastern portion of the country, *kalmer* (a sweet made of pistachio and clotted cream) is sent to the bride's family on the day after the wedding. In small villages along the Black Sea, the bride's family is required to give a second wedding feast ten days after the wedding.

Turkish air force officers salute at Atatürk's mausoleum on Victory Day. This anniversary commemorates the end of the 1922 Greco-Turkish War, an occasion that led to Turkey's independence in 1923.

When a baby is born, the entire community celebrates. Food is brought to the family, and they, in turn, serve frozen sherbet to their guests. In some village traditions, children throw stones at the door of the house where a baby has been born, demanding to see the infant. The father, in order to keep his child, must bribe the youngsters with treats to make them leave. Not surprisingly, Turkish children are enthusiastic about keeping this custom.

## Cultural Festivals

A festival with a more modern origin is Youth and Sports Day, which is celebrated on May 19. It marks the day that Atatürk arrived in Samsun, a port on the Black Sea. When people later looked back at the revolution that ousted the sultan and put Atatürk in power, they considered this day to have been monumental. To celebrate, a statue of Atatürk is carried into the waves by local volunteers, and then carried back out and repositioned to annually commemorate the official beginning of the revolution.

National Sovereignty and Children's Day, a favorite of many schoolchildren, is celebrated on April 23. On this day, children from other countries are invited to come to Turkey to live with a Turkish family for several days. On April 23, the children perform folk dances of their native land, with the Turkish children performing last. One Turkish boy and one Turkish girl are chosen to be "president" of the country for half an hour. They are taken to the president's house and are questioned about what they would do if they were leading the country. Turks also mark Atatürk's death on November 10 with a moment of silence.

# THE RELIGIONS OF TURKEY THROUGHOUT ITS HISTORY

**6**

The majority of Turks are Muslims who practice Islam. Other monotheistic religions, like Judaism and Christianity, are represented by fairly small minority groups—about 2 percent of Turkey's population—and are concentrated in the city of Istanbul.

Islam is the most recent of the world's three major religions. It began in what is now Saudi Arabia with the prophet Muhammad in the seventh century.

## The History of Islam

Muhammad was born around the year AD 572. As an adult, he lived in Mecca and married Khadija, a woman fifteen years older than him. She was a successful businesswoman. For many years, Muhammad and Khadija lived in Mecca, with Muhammad occasionally leaving the city to meditate in a cave called Hira. It was in this cave, at the age of forty, that Muhammad heard a voice ordering him to "Recite!" From this came the name of the book Muhammad eventually wrote, the Koran, also spelled Qur'an, which means "the recitation."

Over the next several years, Muhammad heard the voice many times. He wrote down all that he heard. In the end, he compiled 114 chapters, called suras, or surahs,

Muhammad received the word of the Koran directly from Allah over a twenty-three-year period. This eighteenth-century Islamic painting *(left)* entitled *The Koran Revealed to Muhammad During a Battle* depicts one such revelation. Muslims pray five times a day facing the Saudi Arabian city of Mecca. The removal of shoes *(above)* and washing of hands and feet are rituals of cleanliness that all Muslims must observe.

Displayed in the Musee Conde in Chantilly, France, this page from the Koran is written in calligraphy, the oldest and most common form of Islamic art. Muhammad is never depicted in the Koran, as it is against the practice of Islam to illustrate the holy text with images of man.

that make up the Koran, and another, lesser work of sayings known as the *hadith*, or "the tradition." Muhammad received the suras from the heavenly voice while in a trance.

The first convert to this new faith was Khadija, who enthusiastically supported her husband. He shared his opinions and problems with her; she was his main confidante and friend. Although Muhammad later took other wives, he did not do so until after Khadija's death.

After the death of his wife, Muhammad began having problems with the people of the city. Many of them did not like the new faith he was preaching. In 622, Muhammad fled Mecca toward Yathrib, which is modern-day Medina. This event, called the *hijra*, marks the first year of the Muslim calendar.

Muhammad spent the next ten years communicating his message. In 632, he fell ill and died in the arms of his youngest wife, Aisha. Aisha was the daughter of

Muhammad's close friend Abu Bakr, and in 656, she became a major political figure during a civil war that followed the death of the third caliph. Her role in the early days of Islam was so central that some traditions say the prophet told his followers that they received half of their religion from a woman.

The religion that Muhammad founded centers on the idea of submission to God. God, in Arabic, is Allah, which means "the god." The word "Islam" means "to submit," and a Muslim is considered to be one who submits. The religion recognizes no God but Allah. Muhammad, while he was Allah's prophet, was still only a man.

## The Mark of a Prophet

In Arabia, cats have been considered sacred since the sixth century. The prophet Muhammad loved cats. It is said that the "M" on a tabby's forehead is the mark left by Muhammad's fingers as he stroked a cat on the head. Another story tells of how Muhammad had finished preaching but couldn't leave the mosque because his cat Muezza was asleep in the sleeve of his robe. Instead of waking the cat, he cut off his sleeve so Muezza could continue to sleep undisturbed.

Muslims believe the Koran is the unedited word of God dictated directly to Muhammad. Because of the importance of the words themselves, Koranic texts are written with a short-vowel sign to increase the accuracy of pronunciation. Muslims who are ritually impure should not handle the text at all.

## The Five Pillars

Every Muslim is responsible for upholding the five pillars of the faith. These are fasting during Ramazan, or Ramadan; giving alms (charity) to the poor; making a *hajj*, or pilgrimage, to Mecca; praying five times a day; and reciting the *shahada*, or *shahadah* ("There is no God but Allah and Muhammad is his Prophet").

The *muezzin*, or *mu'adhdhin*, the man who calls Muslims to pray, sings a series of statements of the first seven verses of the Koran. At each daily prayer, the believer is supposed to face toward Mecca, bow his or her head to the floor to show humility before God, and repeat his or her prayers. At the mosque, all male believers stand shoulder to shoulder, no matter their social status, to show that all men are equal before Allah.

Doing good deeds is important in Islam. One story about Muhammad is that he once saw an old man praying all day in the mosque. When he asked how the old

Muezzins call the faithful to prayer from the top of a minaret five times a day, as seen in this drawing. This act is now considered an art form, which is reflected in the chanting of the *adhan*, or prayer.

man supported himself if he only prayed and never worked, someone told the prophet that a merchant who was not religious gave the old man money. Muhammad claimed the man who gave away his money to appease the old man's desire to pray all day was actually the more righteous of the two. The thirty-second verse of the third sura of the Koran says, "By no means shall you attain righteousness unless you give freely of that which you love."

After Muhammad's death, a schism, or religious division, developed among his followers. Abu Bakr was voted the first caliph, or successor, but those who wanted Ali ibn abu Talib, Muhammad's son-in-law, to be the caliph, disputed his rule. This squabble over the succession has continued to divide

## Daily Prayers

The Al-Fatihah is the opening seven-verse chapter of the Koran. It is recited at all prayers. According to devout Muslims, prayer without the Al-Fatihah is considered invalid. "In the name of Allah, Most Gracious, Most Merciful. Praise be to Allah, the Cherisher and Sustainer of the Worlds; Most Gracious, Most Merciful; Master of the Day of Judgment. Thee do we worship. Show us the straight way, the way of those on whom Thou hast bestowed Thy Grace, those whose portion is not wrath, and who go not astray."

This interior view of the Blue Mosque, also known as the Sultan Ahmet Mosque, built between 1609 to 1617, exhibits the architect Sedefkar Mehmet Agha's crafting of this structure to be a spiritual experience.

Muslims into two separate groups to this day.

Those who approved of Abu Bakr as the first caliph became the Sunni sect. Sunni Muslims comprise at least 90 percent of all Muslims. They believe that Muslims should be ruled by consensus through an elected head of state. In contrast to Sunni beliefs, the Shiite tradition says that their ruler should be a descendant of Muhammad himself. Most Muslims in Turkey today are Sunnis.

## The Spread of Islam

The first Turks to become Muslim were the Seljuks. The Seljuk Turks had become mamluks, or slave soldiers, of the empire of the Samanid Persians. At this time, masses of Seljuks converted to Islam. But within

Erected in AD 537, during the reign of the Roman Emperor Justinian, the Great Church, or Megale Ekklesia, was soon known as the Church of Holy Wisdom. In 1453, when the Turks conquered Constantinople, the church was converted to an Islamic mosque known as Hagia Sophia.

## The Monster Tax

During the days of the Ottoman Empire, a substantial number of Christians lived in Istanbul. They paid taxes on their property, including their pigs. Because pork was forbidden for Muslims, the tax collectors called the tax on pigs "the monster tax." To this day, Muslims do not eat pork because they consider it unclean.

two centuries of their conversion and service to the Samanids, the Seljuks took power. This branch of the Seljuks, the Persian Seljuks, quickly adopted the ways of their former masters, living in cities and coming to value artistic creations for their beauty.

Farther west, the Rum Seljuks continued to overrun Anatolia. Their empire lasted from 1073 to 1308, and stretched from Persia in the east to the empire of Nicaea on the Aegean Coast, roughly covering the territory of present-day Turkey.

The Rum Seljuks rejected city life and kept their nomadic ways much longer than the Persian Seljuks did. Some documents claim that even as late as 1200, Rum Seljuk sultans spent their summers in tents outside the walls of their capital city, Konya.

To educate their children and the people they had conquered, the Seljuks built religious schools called *madrasas*. This was largely to keep the population Sunni, since Shiites had attempted to sway people away from Sunni teachings. Therefore, the Seljuks ensured that each town had at least one Koranic school. At the madrasas, the teachers made certain their students learned Islam in what the Seljuks considered to be its purest form. Because religious education was so important to the Seljuks, no expense was spared in building the schools. Architects were free to design large, elaborately decorated buildings.

After the fall of the Seljuk Empire and a century of chaos, the Ottoman Turks formed an empire of their own. They, too, were Sunni Muslims. They spread their religion to Constantinople after its fall in 1453, and then on into Europe through the Balkans and up to the gates of Vienna. Many of the people of southeastern Europe are Muslim to this day because of the once expansive and powerful Ottoman Empire.

## Sufism

One form of Islam that is native to Turkey is Sufism, best known to Westerners as the practice of the whirling dervishes. These people follow the teachings of the Sufi poet Mevlana Celaleddin Rumi, who lived from 1207 to 1273. Sufism is a form of Islam that

This sixteenth-century miniature painting depicts dervishes who feel that dancing and whirling are physical ways to address God. Dervishes are part of the Mevlevi Order, which follows teachings of the poet Mevlana Celaleddin Rumi.

is mystical in nature. Sufis believe that individuals must go beyond formal religious practices to achieve higher levels of spiritual understanding and fulfillment. The word "dervish" is from the Persian *darwish*, which means "doorsill." The term indicates someone who is on the threshold of greater enlightenment.

Rumi was born in modern-day Afghanistan but immigrated to Konya early in his life. He preached a form of Islam that advocated tolerance of others, charity, goodness, and love for all people. He turned no one away, writing, "Come, whoever you are, come. Even if you broke your penitence a hundred times, ours is the portal of hope. Come as you are."

An important aspect of the devotion of the followers of Sufism—members of the Order of Dervishes—is a dance called *sema*. Because the dance involves turning in circles, the word "whirling" has been applied to followers of Rumi.

Moving in circles represents a spiritual journey toward that which is perfect. The descendants of Rumi say that the believer will "return from this spiritual journey as a man who reached maturity and a greater perfection, so as to love and to be of service to the whole of creation, to all creatures without discrimination of beliefs, races, classes, and nations." Today, the town of Konya is the center of Sufism in Turkey and also host to the annual Mevlana Festival, which commemorates the death of Mevlana Celaleddin Rumi on December 17, 1273.

## Religion in Modern Turkey

Though the modern Republic of Turkey is a secular (nonreligious) state, the government funds religious schools and mosques. Yet Atatürk's reforms were partly to ensure that the

In Istanbul, a whirling dervish dances in order to be closer to God. Dervishes usually dance to music of reed flutes, hand drums, and the Turkish fiddle.

people of Turkey would live their lives free of strict religious laws. Sufism, in fact, often came under attack as an example of outmoded religious thinking in Turkish society. Eventually, this lack of support pushed the Order of Dervishes underground. Atatürk made it illegal to wear religious clothing in public. He outlawed traditional items like the fez, and he encouraged women to give up their veils.

## The Role of Women

Today, Atatürk's vision for Turkey seems to be forgotten. Because past secular reforms had alienated Muslims, many religious Turks want to push the country toward more traditional laws and practices. Other people have become alarmed at the growing trend for women to take up the veil once again. In a land where women have been holding public office since 1934, and a female prime minister was chosen in 1993, this swing back to more orthodox religious practices concerns many residents.

Early converts to Islam were often women; Khadija and Aisha are only two examples. And Aisha's powerful influence during a civil war indicates that women were not always as separated from politics in Islam as they are in some places today.

Muhammad ensured that women—who, up until that time in Arabia, were often considered no more important than animals—were seen as dignified. Although men and women were not necessarily equal before the law, they were equal before Allah. Women were assured the right to own property and be educated. Aisha herself was literate and respected for her intellect.

The earliest practice of Islam did not allow women equality under religious law. A woman could not divorce her husband without a court order, while her husband could divorce her without one. In court, a woman's testimony was only worth half as much as a man's testimony, and a woman's portion of the family inheritance was half as much as her brother's.

Muslims study the Koran in order to achieve both a personal and scholarly interpretation of the text. It is considered a tradition for Muslims to memorize its passages.

Over the centuries, various societies have differed in their interpretations of the role of women in Islamic society. In Turkey during the Ottoman Empire, women were often relegated to the harem and not involved in political life. They were usually illiterate and uneducated, yet even so, some women, like Lady Mihri, learned to read and write and even became well-known poets.

After the founding of the Republic of Turkey, women advanced quickly. Atatürk wrote in 1925, "A society, a nation is made up of both sexes, male and female. Is it ever possible that we only improve one part of this mass and leave the other part aside if we expect the whole nation to improve? Is it ever possible for a society to be divided in two and to raise up to the skies while half of it is chained to the ground?"

Those who wish a return to a more orthodox state of Islam are called Islamists. Those who support the secular establishment—such as teachers, businesses, banks, the tourist trade, the older political parties, the media, and many civic groups— oppose Islamists. Yet, as Marvine Howe relates in her book *Turkey Today*, "Little by little, Islamists are in the process of creating what amounts to a parallel society." It is impossible to predict how the tension between the supporters of the secular society envisioned by Atatürk and the Islamists will be resolved.

# THE ART AND ARCHITECTURE OF TURKEY

**7**

Although the art of Turkey is rich and diverse, all Turkish expression is influenced by the tenets of Islam. Because the religion does not allow for the representation of the human figure, most Turkish art takes the form of floral motifs and intricate patterns.

## Ceramic Arts

One of the finest representations of Turkish artisanship can be found in its ceramic arts. With kilns dating back to the seventeenth century, tiles were often produced by master potters in the city of Iznik and used throughout the Ottoman Empire to adorn the walls and ceilings of mosques as well as the homes of nobles and private citizens. Famous for their quality and beauty, Iznik tiles are today renowned as important works of Turkish art. Examples of Iznik tiles may be found in Istanbul's famous Blue Mosque.

Most architecture seen in Turkey today came from the Ottoman Empire. The most impressive of these structures are the great mosques in Istanbul.

## Hagia Sophia

Perhaps the most famous building in Istanbul is the Hagia Sophia (Aya Sofya, or Saint Sophia) or the Church of Holy Wisdom, originally a Christian cathedral. Once the world's largest enclosed space, it was built by the architects Isidorus and Anthemius in five years from 532 to 537, during the reign of the roman emperor Justinian. Both men

Muslims worship inside the Süleymaniye Mosque *(left)* in Edirne, Turkey. Ottoman architect Sinan built the mosque in the 1570s for Sultan Selim II. A Turkish potter *(above)* hand-paints a bowl in Cappadocia, a region known for its fine-quality pottery.

Iznik tiles decorate Topkapi Palace's circumcision room in the harem wing. Admired worldwide, Iznik tile is popular for its hard composition of the semiprecious stone quartz, which gives the tile a turquoise, red, or emerald color.

were born in Anatolia, and Isidorus most likely studied architecture and engineering in Constantinople. Anthemius is believed to have studied in Alexandria, Egypt. The architects borrowed from several traditions to form a new style of architecture that is now called Byzantine. Intricate mosaic tiles often adorn this style, which features domes supported by triangular arches over a square space. In 563, the original dome of the Hagia Sophia collapsed in an earthquake and was replaced.

After the fall of Constantinople to the Ottomans in 1453 and the emergence of Islam in the region, a new era of building projects was inaugurated. Although the Byzantine edifices left behind by their Christian predecessors impressed the Ottomans, the Hagia Sophia was altered to reflect Islamic traditions. The church was converted into a mosque and four minarets were added. Today, the building is a museum.

The sultan who conquered Constantinople, Mehmed II, brought scholars, engineers, artists, and architects to the city so that he could continue his education. Interestingly, many of these educated men came from Christian kingdoms, for despite having conquered Constantinople, Mehmed II, whose mother had been Christian, was not interested in suppressing Christianity. Mehmed II was open to outside cultures and religions and wanted the world's most advanced knowledge to influence his court. In fact, the cannons that shot down the walls of Constantinople during the siege had been built by German ironsmiths.

Mehmed eventually decided to build a great mosque on the site of the ruins of the Church of the Holy Apostles. That church had originally been constructed

during the reign of Justinian, but unlike the Hagia Sophia, it had not survived the intervening nine centuries. The sultan chose a Christian architect, Christodoulos, who was known to the Ottomans as Atik Sinan, or "The Elder Sinan," to differentiate him from a later architect of the same name.

Atik Sinan's work was the Mosque of the Conqueror, or the Fatih Camii. It was built between 1463 and 1471, but was destroyed by an earthquake in 1766. Excavations have revealed that its design was partially influenced by the Hagia Sophia.

Other great works of the Ottomans have survived to modern times, such as the Fiezade, built during the reign of Süleyman the Magnificent (1520–1566) by Mimar Sinan.

Hagia Sophia's four minarets were added after the Turks invaded Constantinople and converted the church into a mosque. Since 1923, the structure has been a museum. At that time, Atatürk, the leader of the Republic of Turkey, replaced older Islamic laws with a Swiss-based civil code in order to limit Islam's influence over the Turks. "The Republic of Turkey cannot be the land of sheikhs, dervishes, disciples, and lay brothers," he said.

Mimar Sinan had been one of the Christian boys collected by the devflirme and had been inducted into the Janissaries. His intelligence and early work on military fortifications brought him to the attention of Süleyman; soon after, Mimar Sinan was appointed to the sultan's court of personal care assistants. When he was fifty years old, in 1539, he was appointed Süleyman's chief architect.

The Fiezade was the first great architectural work Sinan was assigned after his new appointment. The name comes from the Persian term *shah zadeh* and means "the crown prince." Süleyman also had a mosque built in the memory of his favorite son. Scholars argue about the exact date, but the mosque was begun somewhere near 1543. But even before it was finished, Süleyman had Sinan begin working on another, even grander, mosque—the Süleymaniye.

## Süleymaniye Mosque

Both the Süleymaniye and Fiezade Mosques stand under central domes that are buttressed by other domes. The central dome of the Süleymaniye rises 174 feet (53 meters) above the floor and is 87 feet (26.5 meters) across, applying a strict Islamic canon of geometry that doubles a mosque's height by two times its width. Intricate designs with striped arches and colored tiles adorn this Istanbul wonder, while its four spiked minarets stand out from the rest of the city's skyline. Ibrahim the Drunkard designed its 200 glass windows, many of them colorful stained glass.

Located on the Golden Horn of the West Bank in Istanbul, the Süleymaniye Mosque was built between 1550 and 1557 by renowned Ottoman architect Mimar Sinan. In its garden complex, Süleyman and his wife constructed their mausoleum.

Because of the Muslim proscription against rendering animal or human forms in art, the walls of the Süleymaniye Mosque are covered in beautiful flowers, geometric designs, and passages from the Koran. These spiritual verses, which are written in Arabic, are rendered in an ornamental penmanship called calligraphy, one of Turkey's oldest visual art forms.

Between the fifteenth and the eighteenth centuries, Topkapi Palace was the focal point of the Ottoman Empire. Today, the palace houses museums specific to archaeology and Islamic art.

## Topkapi Palace

While Turkey's spirituality is often expressed in the heart of its beautiful mosques, the splendor and power of the Ottoman Empire can be best illustrated in the design of the Topkapi Palace. This series of fifteenth-century buildings is where the sultan and his wives, children, and court lived. The area where the women resided was the 250-room harem, now a favorite visiting spot for tourists who are curious about a private space where 1,000 people—women, children, and concubines—once lived. The area where men lived was called the *selamlik*.

Topkapi Palace was begun under the reign of Mehmed II, but later sultans added buildings to suit their own tastes. As a result, the buildings within the palace walls reflect various architectural periods. The entrance to Topkapi Palace is through the Gate of Perpetual Delight, which is often called the Imperial Gate. Within this entryway are spacious courtyards, kiosks, and libraries. One of the few surviving kiosks is the Sepetciler Kiosk, built in 1643 by the Sultan Ibrahim.

Many of the courtyards of Topkapi are covered in intricate designs made by placing different colored pebbles or tiles into patterns. This mosaic art form, the work of master craftsmen, was popularized in the Byzantine Empire and later adopted by the Ottoman Turks.

The Gate of Salutation, through which only the sultan was allowed to pass on horseback, guards the inner courtyard of the palace. Everyone else had to walk. Even farther within the structure are the third and fourth courts, which are reached only through narrow corridors. These areas, hidden away from the court, were reserved for the sultan to relax. They contain kiosks, gardens, fountains, pools, and even a marble terrace overlooking the inlet known as the Golden Horn.

The palace is also known for housing many art objects from the height of Ottoman rule, including a cache of miniature paintings and the Topkapi dagger.

## Yalis

During the eighteenth century, it became fashionable for nobles living in Istanbul to build houses along the waterfront. At first, sultans gave out plots of prime waterfront land only to close family members, but as time went on, other members of the elite were able to acquire this land to build their summer retreats. Competition erupted between the noblemen to see who could have the biggest house, the most fountains, or the most beautiful gardens.

These houses are called *yalis*, from the Greek word *yialos*, which means "seashore." Today, many yalis still line the waterfront near Istanbul. The oldest standing structure is the Köprülü Amcazade Hüseyin Pafla yali, which was erected in 1698. Most early yalis were built of wood and colored in a dark rust-red called Ottoman rose. Today, many yalis still retain this color, though later the style moved more toward pastel exteriors.

The design of every yali is similar. The central hall goes entirely through the house so that one can walk from the front door to windows overlooking the water. The yali has four corner rooms off this central corridor.

Having separate rooms was essential for the upper-class Ottoman family. Even husbands and wives ate dinner separately. Female guests were received in the harem, while male guests were received in the selamlik. Cooking was done by servants in an outside building. Today, distinctions between men's quarters and women's quarters are no longer made. Even before the Republic of Turkey was founded, the strict separation of sexes was slowly being eroded. By the early twentieth century, women could be found attending parties in the gardens of the selamlik.

Count Ostrorog, a polish nobleman who served as legal consultant to the Ottoman Empire, built the home shown in this photograph, the Ostrorog yali. It dates from the nineteenth century and is the "Ottoman rose" color popular at the time.

The interiors of the yalis were decorated much like Topkapi Palace. Rooms of tile, inlay, marble, and carved wood were common. All forms of extravagance, from gold to elaborately painted frescoes, were used to make the yali grand.

Elsewhere in Turkey, buildings mimic the style the sultans adopted in Istanbul. The Yepil Camii (Green Mosque) in Bursa, for instance, has its walls and ceiling entirely covered in gold mosaics.

# Theater

Turkish popular theater can be grouped into three main types: the *Orta oiunu* (middle play), the *Meddah*, and *Karagöz*.

Orta oiunu is called the middle play because it requires a great deal of open space to stage. Thus, it was usually performed in a town square or in the middle of a field. During the Ottoman Empire, the sultan kept a company of court actors to perform for special occasions. Women sat in a special section of the audience that was set off by veils. That way, members of the harem could watch the plays privately.

The parts in an Orta oiunu are standardized and are usually stereotypical. The main performer is called Pishekiar; he is a clever man. He always begins the play and rarely leaves the stage. The secondary character is called Kavuklu, which means "with a large wadded hat." He may be a trader or a servant. Most of the play's dialogue takes place between Pishekiar and Kavuklu.

Zenne is a character who signifies any female role, though men traditionally play female characters. Zampara is often a heroic character. Other actors represent ethnic groups: Kaisarli is a man from the district of Kaisariye, Ermeni is an Armenian, Arnaut is an Albanian, and Adjem is a Persian.

The Meddah form of theater was borrowed from the Arabs. Meddahs are storytellers. The beginning of the performance consists of the storyteller reciting a religious text or proverb. From that, he begins his tale. Although this form of entertainment was popular, it often came under censorship. During the nineteenth century, for instance, Meddahs

After the sunset meal during the fasting month of Ramadan, Turks watch musicians perform as the comedic characters of the Karagöz shadow-puppet theater. This performance is a traditional Ottoman show.

Master puppeteers perform in Istanbul. Festivities such as this date from the time of the Ottoman Empire when acrobatics, juggling, fireworks, and theatrical reenactment of battles in shadow play celebrated the circumcision of the sultans' sons.

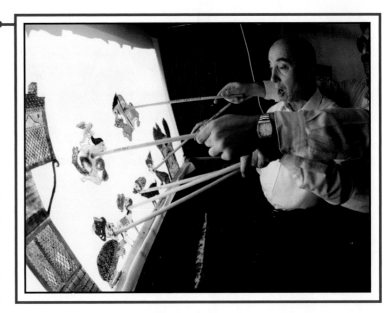

were forbidden to use the word "sultan" or to criticize the government.

By the nineteenth century, Meddahs performed less for the court and more for the public. The storyteller continually changed his repertoire of tales so that he never repeated the same one exactly. Because of this, texts of Meddah tales are very rare. The changing nature of the tales was considered part of their charm.

## Shadow Puppetry

The third kind of popular theater in Turkey is called Karagöz, which means "black-eyed," the name of the principal character. Karagöz is a shadow puppet, usually performed by one puppeteer who must speak all the dialogue and sing the songs.

Most of each shadow-puppet play consists of dialogue between Karagöz and his friend Hacivat. Karagöz represents the common person. He is a simple, crude character, but he has a great wit and can sometimes be quite cunning. He makes many jokes. Sometimes he is punished, but he always wins in the end. Hacivat is a pompous character who uses pretentious language and is mocked by Karagöz. The audience loves to see Karagöz make fun of his haughty friend and is always eager to see him emerge victorious by the end of the production.

# THE LITERATURE AND MUSIC OF TURKEY

## 8

**D**uring the time of the Hittites, two main forms of literature existed in Asia Minor. The first was hymns of praise to the gods. The other was the Hittite law code.

## Ancient Law Codes

Hittite law codes covered a wide range of subjects. Many of those subjects were administrative in nature, such as keeping records of slave and marriage contracts as well as records of inheritance of property and even early forms of ancient medicine, which was more like magic. For instance, it was illegal for a man to kill a snake and say another person's name at the same time. If the man who did this was free, he would be fined. If he were a slave, he would be killed. The Hittites believed that killing the snake while invoking the person's name would bring bad luck or even death to that person. They wanted to ensure that anyone caught trying to harm another person would be punished.

Law codes were also important to Justinian, an emperor of the Byzantine Empire who ruled from 527 to 565. At the time, there were two kinds of Roman law: *jus vetus* ("old law") and *jus novum* ("new law"). By the time of Justinian, these law codes

Dated 1610, this Turkish miniature painting *(left)* housed at the Topkapi Palace Museum in Istanbul, Turkey, shows a festival of musicians honoring the sultan. An eighteenth-century watercolor on paper *(above)* by Ottoman artist Levni depicts concert musicians.

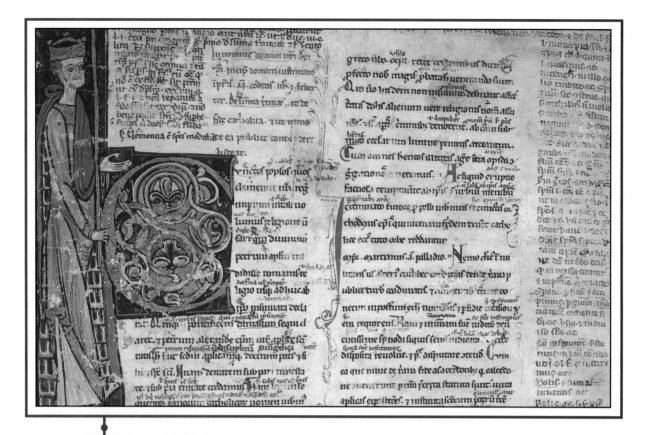

In the sixth century, Emperor Justinian implemented a set of laws, called the Codex Justinianus, which regulated society's behavior through legal procedures. As the principles of the codex became established, the laws ultimately influenced other ancient societies, including the Roman Empire.

were a confused, contradictory mess. Justinian assigned lawyers the task of updating the jus novum into a cohesive law code in 528; shortly thereafter, the Codex Justinianus was produced. Then Justinian's people set to work on the jus vetus, which was much longer and more complex. The final fifty-volume work was called the *Digest*. The West did not discover Justinian's work until after 1100. Once discovered, this code that was written during the Byzantine Empire, in Turkey, would contribute enormously to the future law codes of Europe.

## The Ottoman Empire

During the Byzantine Empire, most people could not read or write. Those who could were most concerned with recording information about laws and collected revenues, as well as holy texts. But once the Ottoman Turks conquered the area, the recording of written information drastically changed.

The Ottoman Turks had converted to Islam during their migration more than a thousand years ago, and the Islamic world was educated and literate. An Islamic gentleman was expected to be polite, well read, and versed in subjects like poetry. Universities like the one in Baghdad taught many subjects, including medicine. Islamic doctors even attempted to relieve their patients' stress with music.

Because literacy, and especially a knowledge of poetry, was considered important, many men of the upper classes in the Ottoman Empire had learned to read. Some of them wrote poems that are still available today.

Most Ottoman literature can be described as belonging to one of five various categories: *aflick*, or poetry sung by traveling minstrels; *divan*, which was derived from Persian sources; secular writings of scientists and other scholars; religious tracts; and plays and novels written for entertainment.

## Ottoman Writers

Ahmedi (1334–1413) was a divan poet of the fourteenth century. Though Ahmedi was a poet, he was also a scientist and a physician. His major poem is called *The Iskandername*, which consists of 10,000 verses about the heroic deeds of his patron's ancestors. Ahmedi was one of the first divan poets to write in the Turkish language rather than in Persian, which for years was the only language for court poetry.

Yunus Emre (1250–1320) was another famous Turkish poet, and one who spent much of his life wandering around Asia Minor and Syria. Emre traveled as far as the Caucasus Mountains, a natural range rising between the Black and Caspian Seas, marking the separation between Europe and Asia. He continues to be popular to this day, so much that several towns claim to be his birthplace. Today, Emre's writings are still considered to be a model of pure Turkish language and lyrical style. One of his famous poems contains the line, "Let us love, let us be loved, no one has here for long to stay."

One famous female poet was Lady Mihri (died 1506), the daughter of a judge. Her poems, often emphasizing simplicity, still seem surprisingly modern. One of her poems contains the line, "One female who knows what to do is better than a thousand males who don't."

Women poets, however, were rare in Turkey. Because literacy skills were not valued in women, it was only in rare circumstances that a noblewoman managed to convince her father to allow her to become literate.

Ahmet Mithat (1844–1912) was an Ottoman writer who worked as a journalist. In 1873, he was given three years exile for an editorial he wrote. When he finally returned to Turkey in 1877, he published the newspaper *Tercüman-i Hakikat*. His works include some of the first Turkish science fiction and detective stories, though he also wrote novels and plays. Mithat did not feel he wrote anything terribly important; he once said, "Neither my time nor my pen have sufficed to produce literature."

## Modern Writers

After the founding of the republic, literacy rates climbed as more people went to school. Atatürk envisioned a Turkey with literacy rates comparable to the West. He also wanted everyone to be literate, including women. Because of his reforms, many twentieth-century authors of Turkey have been women.

As more people became educated, different schools of literature appeared. In the 1950s, the Ikinci Yeni, or "Second New" school of poetry developed. This writing has been compared to the "beat" poetry going on in the West around the same time.

More serious literature, including realistic short stories depicting the grim realities of life in rural areas, also appeared. What made this new crop of work different from earlier eras was that many of the authors were peasants who had grown up living in the conditions they described. Prior to the founding of the republic, government policies toward rural areas were sometimes criticized, but only by the educated elite, not by the people themselves, who were illiterate.

Haiku—a form of Japanese poetry—influenced popular Turkish writer Orhan Veli Kanik, who sought to break the conventional mold of polite Turkish verse and abandoned its more common rhyme and meter tradition.

Orhan Veli Kanik (1914–1950) was one of the most important Turkish writers of the twentieth century. Kanik believed it was important to "free ourselves from poetic conceptions." In his free verse, he drew more inspiration from Japanese poetry like haiku than from traditional Turkish styles. He discarded rhyme and meter. Near the end of his life, he published a literary journal called *Yaprak* (Leaf).

Halide Edip Adivar (also spelled Adyvar), with Mustafa Kemal Atatürk, led the emancipation of women in Turkey and dedicated herself to the improvement of educational conditions for women. Through her writings of social and political topics, Adivar advocated for change in women's roles in Turkey.

## Halide Edip Adivar

Perhaps the most famous woman author of modern Turkey was Halide Edip Adivar (1881–1955). Many of her works were originally published in English. Although she was born during the time of the Ottoman Empire when women were not educated, Adivar's father believed his daughter should read and write. Eventually, she attended college and continued her education with private tutors. Later she worked with Atatürk during World War I and was commissioned as a sergeant major in the Turkish army, serving on the general staff. After the war, however, she and Atatürk had a falling out and Adivar and her husband were banished for fifteen years. Adivar left Turkey for the United States, where she began studying at New York's Columbia University. Once there, Adivar gave lectures on Turkish literature and wrote her most well-known novel, *The Clown and His Daughter*. She returned to Turkey after Atatürk's death and accepted a position as professor of English at the University of Istanbul. Several of Adivar's books have been adapted into Turkish films.

## Ihsani the Minstrel

Echoes of the past can still be found in Turkey. Ihsani the Minstrel was born in 1930 to a poor family originally from Iran. His father rebelled against the local landlord and was killed when Ihsani was a child. As a result, he grew up as an outcast in extreme poverty. As an adult, Ihsani wandered the countryside like the aflick poets of the Ottoman Empire. His songs concerned the social injustices he experienced in his own life and the ones he observed on his travels. The critical tone of his songs and poems sometimes got him arrested, though he was never sentenced to prison. His poetry includes works with titles like "Vur a Danyn Bapyna" ("Hit the Boss on the Head").

## Fazil Hüsnü Daglarca

Fazil Hüsnü Daglarca was born in 1914. He was first published in 1933, when he was nineteen years old. He continued to write and publish poetry during his career as an army officer. In 1967, the International Poetry Forum selected Daglarca as the best Turkish poet. Later, at the Thirteenth Struga in Yugoslavia, he was awarded a golden wreath for poetry in 1974. Daglarca's contemporary use of language and clear, descriptive voice make him one of Turkey's most beloved and well known poets.

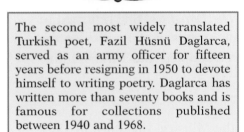

The second most widely translated Turkish poet, Fazil Hüsnü Daglarca, served as an army officer for fifteen years before resigning in 1950 to devote himself to writing poetry. Daglarca has written more than seventy books and is famous for collections published between 1940 and 1968.

# Folk Music

The Turks who migrated to Anatolia brought their traditional folk music with them. This music expressed the feelings and beliefs of nomads who sang about love, sorrow, and happiness. Tunes were adopted by many different traveling groups and then altered over time so that many variations of these traditional folk songs can be found today.

Most folk music in Turkey can be grouped in one of two categories: *Kirk Havalar*, which uses rhythm in its melodies; and *Uzun Havalar*, which does not. Folk music of this type is often limited to a range of one to one-and-a-half octaves, which most untrained singers can reach easily.

In 1925, Seyfettin and Sezai Azal traveled the country collecting traditional folk songs. They published their collection as *Tunes of Our Country*. Over the next several decades, many trips were taken by music conservators into rural areas of Turkey to collect and record traditional music. The Ankara State Conservatory has collected well over 10,000 melodies, many of which have now been recorded.

This musician plays a traditional Turkish instrument called a *saz* on the Galata Bridge in the Eminonu district in Istanbul. The Yeni Camii Mosque can be seen in the background.

## Instruments

The instruments that are used in folk music are often small and portable, which hearkens back to the days when people had to carry their instruments with them. Common instruments such as the *kemençe*, which resembles a fiddle, or the *ud*, which resembles a lute, are three-stringed and are plucked rather than strummed. Wind instruments, such as the *tulum* or *mey*, are made of bone or reeds. Percussion instruments include the *davul* drum, cymbals, and the *kasik*, which is a set of wooden or metal spoons.

# Court Music

The tunes of the common people were never found at the court of the Ottoman sultans. In the educated and Persian-influenced atmosphere of the court, many musical styles were developed. Nobles were often the patrons of court musicians if they were not musicians themselves. Many sultans even tried their hand at writing music.

Ali Ufki Bey, a Pole who converted to Islam in 1640, collected more than 400 songs and wrote them down using musical notation. Before Bey, songs were learned by memorization but were not transcribed. For this reason, his work is

significant. The musicians at court now had a way to write down their songs for future generations.

Sultans had their own band, the *Mehter* band, which was composed of Janissaries. However, when Mahmud II disbanded the Janissaries in 1826, he adopted the custom of having a Western-style brass band for his use. Beginning with this sultan, the use and promotion of traditional court music declined in favor of Western styles.

Mahmud's foray into Western music was not the first for a sultan. In 1543, the first European orchestra to visit Istanbul was sent by King Francois I of France to the court of Süleyman the Magnificent. Süleyman enjoyed the Western music so much that he ordered his musicians to compose similar works. The resulting Frenkisi style remained popular until the end of the empire.

By the end of the nineteenth century, court music spread to the rest of the country. Haci Emin (1845–1907), a music publisher, printed the first music notation books in 1876. And the first state-established music conservatory, the Daru'I-Elhan, was founded in 1917. After the beginning of the republic, the conservatory's name was changed to the Istanbul Municipality Conservatory.

Today, many popular musicians in Turkey utilize Western pop forms in their music, but with a Turkish flavor, while composers of classical music write Western-styled symphonies with Turkish melodies. Turkey represents a synthesis of East and West, especially in its music.

Military *Mehter* music accompanied the marching Ottoman army into battle. Its sounds signified the strength, courage, and independence of the soldiers. Today, the Ottoman Mehter marching band gives concerts throughout Istanbul during Ramadan.

# FAMOUS FOODS AND RECIPES OF TURKEY

## 9

The Turkish people enjoy food so thoroughly that they have even composed poetry and ballads in its honor. This is because, for Turks, eating is part of an overall sense of community. Turkish families gather together over leisurely meals that often last for hours at a time. When friends gather together in restaurants, they frequently talk the evening away. And special events like marriages and births are celebrated with feasts that last for several days.

## Borrowed Foods

In the days when the Turks were nomadic, they ate a great deal of meat. Sometimes they even cured the meat by hanging it from their saddles and letting the wind dry it as it was preserved by the salt from their horses' sweat. Besides meat, nomads prepared dairy items like yogurt and butter. Whenever possible, the Turks gathered—but did not plant—grains such as barley and wheat. They drank *kymyz*, which is fermented mare's milk.

Food preparation was simple during ancient times. The Turks had adopted the wok from China and called it *çin tavasy*. In these shallow pots, they made pastas called *manty*, which are similar to the Chinese dumplings known as wonton, which are familiar to Americans today. Meat was often skewered on sticks; an

A Kurdish family pounds bulgur *(left)*, a parched, cracked wheat, which is a staple in Turkey. Bulgur is used in nearly every dish, including soup, pilaf, salad, desserts, and drinks. One of the oldest known Turkish desserts is baklava *(above)*, a sweet, flaky pastry. A serving of baklava for dessert often follows traditional Turkish meals.

A man makes *doner kebabs*. Doner kebabs are a popular Turkish food consisting of minced lamb, herbs, and spices, which are pressed into a conical shape using animal fat and egg.

eleventh-century Turkish dictionary lists the term for this as *pip kebab*. Many people in the United States today eat grilled, skewered meat, call it shish kebab, and never know they are using a word that originated with the Turks.

After they settled in Asia Minor, the Turks adopted foods and customs from surrounding areas. They learned about rice from the Persians, and enjoyed eating seafood like the Greeks. Items such as olives, cabbage, and chickpeas, which were already being grown in Asia Minor, were added to the typical Turkish diet.

## Royal Menus

During the reign of Mehmed II, known as the Conqueror, hundreds of cooks were hired to work in the kitchens of Topkapi Palace. The cooks competed with each other to devise new and delicious dishes for the pleasure of the sultan, his family, and his guests. The inhabitants of the palace loved food so much that a poet of the time, Bushak, wrote many poems about the subject. One of them is called "Dream of Being in a Tomb Made of Food." Another is called "Ballad of Pilav with Saffron and Börek." *Börek* is a kind of Turkish pastry. *Pilav* is usually spelled pilaf in the United States

The cooks of Topkapi Palace seized on new and exciting recipes. The trade routes of the Silk Road provided exotic ingredients from the Far East. Trade with Italy brought new dishes from the West. By the time of Süleyman the

Magnificent, the cooks had their own six-domed kitchen, and the sultan's family had twelve chefs and two hundred assistants.

Built in 1664, this spice market in Istanbul is a popular tourist attraction. Scents of coffee, vanilla, and cloves typically fill nearby streets.

## Meze

One custom that originated during the Ottoman Empire that is still followed today is that of the *meze*. Meze is a Persian word that means "pleasurable taste," and it represents a meal where small bowls of many different kinds of food are offered. People will often spend entire evenings sharing one dish after another, sampling everything. This custom began when the sultans of the empire hired food tasters to certify that their food was free from poisons. The food tasters were given small samples of all the dishes the sultan requested.

Typical meze dishes include *salatasi*, which is a carrot salad; *fava*, a mashed brown bean salad; and *pastyrma*, which Westerners call pastrami. Meze is typically eaten with *raky*, an alcoholic drink made from raisins that tastes like anise.

# Turkish Delight

The word for Turkish delight—*lokum*—is derived from *rahat loukoum*, which means "rest for the throat." These gummy sugar cubes are served after dinner and are one of the oldest confections in the world, originating from the Ottoman Empire.

Servings: 6
Cooking time: approx. 1 hour

2 1/2 cups water
4 cups sugar
1 cup cornstarch
3/4 cup grape, orange, or lemon juice
1 teaspoon cream of tartar
Food coloring (optional)
Bowl of powdered sugar

Bring water to boil.
Add sugar and stir thoroughly until dissolved.
Mix cornstarch with juice and cream of tartar.
Gradually pour mixture into boiling syrup, stirring constantly.
Cook for 20 minutes, stirring frequently to prevent sticking.
Add food coloring.

Oil a 7-inch square cake pan.
Pour in mixture. Let stand to cool until set, possibly overnight. (Mixture should feel soft but firm after cooling.)
Cut into 1-inch squares.
Dust with powdered sugar and serve.
Store any uneaten pieces in an airtight container.

A street vendor in Istanbul sells *simit*, a traditional and inexpensive bread. Ottoman bakers thought that Adam, patron saint of bakers, learned bread-making from the Archangel Gabriel, a belief that modern bakers also hold true.

## Modern Meals

While two meals were a daily standard for most Turks during the days of the Ottoman Empire, Turks today usually eat three meals. Breakfast, which is generally eaten early in the morning, is called *sabahlary,* or *kahvalty*. It usually consists of bread, white cheese, and jam or honey. Breakfast may be supplemented with cold boiled eggs, vegetables, or some meat or soup. Beverages for breakfast normally include hot tea. Lunch, which is eaten around noon, is also light fare, if the main meal is to be eaten at night, or can be much more elaborate. Sweets like *börek* or other pastries are consumed late in the afternoon.

Dinner is usually the main meal of the day. Families will often eat after sundown and spend their evenings over many courses. Food is customarily served lukewarm rather than hot. Typical courses may include soup, salad, vegetables, meats, and rice. Two courses of dessert are not uncommon.

Between meals, snacks like cobs of corn, ice cream, and *simit* (bread ring) are available from street vendors. Turkish ice cream is not the same thing as in the United States; it is thick, ropy, and very chewy.

The Turkish habit of adopting foreign foods means it is now possible to eat anything from tacos to chocolate chip cookies in Turkey. But instead of replacing local fare, the new foods are normally added to traditional Turkish menus.

# DAILY LIFE AND CUSTOMS IN TURKEY

**10**

Family life in Turkey is much the same as it is in the United States. Turks are a diverse people who share religious customs but have varied lifestyles. Most Turks still live in the rural countryside. Other Turks, who once lived largely in agricultural areas, today live in cities such as Istanbul, many of them in apartments. Turks drive or take buses to work, and most work Monday through Friday from morning until late afternoon.

The changes wrought by Atatürk meant that women became a larger part of the workforce. Professions of all types are available to modern Turkish women, including the fields of medicine, engineering, and architecture. Many women now attend universities.

Family sizes are often small in Turkey, and on average, Turkish women have one or two children. Extended families sometimes live close together; for instance, grandparents may reside in the same apartment building as their children and grandchildren, but normally extended families live apart.

Young people date whom they wish, and often meet their future spouses in college. In many cases, both spouses will work outside the home after marriage.

Average Turkish families may enjoy taking vacations to the seaside and often devote at least two weeks every year to vacation. Antalya and Izmir are two popular

Istanbul annually receives 200,000 migrants from the countryside *(left)* as a result of a lack of jobs in Turkey's rural areas. However, the industrial city is having a difficult time accommodating its rapidly growing population with totals that have increased from about one million to more than nine million people over the past half century. Currently, Istanbul has 1.5 million registered vehicles, 16,000 businesses, and 303 newspapers. A man selects food from the spice market in Istanbul *(above)*.

destinations as are the Hot Springs of Pamukkale, which have been popular since Roman times.

In the past, government workers have been able to take advantage of special resorts called *kamps*. These places were not luxurious, but offered inexpensive lodging and buffet meals. Kamps were located at different tourist destinations around the country. Since Turkey's economic troubles of the past few years, however, the government has begun to abandon such benefits.

## Urban Life

Like many cosmopolitan European cities, Istanbul and Ankara are densely populated. With a constant influx of new residents—estimated figures show more than 250,000 each year—transportation and housing are a constant and ongoing problem. Squatters, or people who establish temporary residences in these cities, are not uncommon. Overcrowding has also led to a unique kind of transportation system

called the *dolmus*: a car or mini bus, much like a taxi, but with a systematic route that picks up and drops off residents throughout a major city. Often, Turks flock to urban areas to find work that cannot be found in the countryside.

The New Galata Bridge in Istanbul is the longest bascule, or counter-balanced, bridge in the world. Constructed in 1994 after the previous Galata Bridge was destroyed by fire, the New Galata is the main connection across the Bosporous.

## Leisure

Sports are very popular in Turkey, where many people are fans of soccer. Basketball is also gaining in popularity, and the Turkish team is ranked seventh-best overall of the European teams that have competed from 1957 to today.

Wrestling is a time-honored sport in Turkey, with many athletes wrestling professionally. Still, many Turks wrestle for fun at county fairs. To make it difficult for opponents to get a good hold, most wrestlers in Turkey grease their skin with olive oil. Every year a greased wrestling festival is held in the city of Edirne.

Although Turkey's most popular sport remains soccer, one ancient and traditional sport called *cirit* still survives today.

Cirit was originally a means for young men to improve their riding skills, an important ability since the days when Turks were nomadic and forced to fight on horseback. Today, the training for these young men survives in the form of a game.

During the Ottoman Empire, cirit was extremely popular. It was even played in between battles so that the cavalry could practice its attack and defense skills and also boost its morale. Experienced cirit players were advanced to a special part of the cavalry called the *cündi*.

*Cirit*, an equestrian sport where competitors must hit each other with javelins, takes specialized skills that are sometimes passed from father to son.

In the early days of the empire, even sultans played the game; however, because it was so dangerous, cirit was eventually banned by Mahmud II shortly after he destroyed the Janissaries in 1826.

Cirit is most popular today around Erzurum. Sometimes, tournaments are organized or games are played for tourists. The game itself is simple: Each player has a blunt stick made of oak or poplar. Two teams on horseback line up facing each other about 300 feet (100 meters) apart. Prior to the game, the players on each team are introduced to the spectators while bands play folk tunes and crowds cheer.

Traditionally, the youngest member opens the game and rides toward the opposing team. When he is within range, he throws his stick at his opponents. He then turns his horse and gallops back to his own line while one of his opponents follows and tries to hit him with his own thrown stick. The horses used in the game are specially trained to wheel and run quickly.

The object of the game is to try to hit your opponents with sticks while avoiding being hit with one yourself. Because today's sticks are lightweight, injuries are few. During Ottoman times, the sticks were heavy and many injuries—some fatal—occurred.

At home, people play games like chess and backgammon as they do in the United States. Card games are also popular.

# EDUCATION AND WORK IN TURKEY

I n the days when Turkey was part of the Ottoman Empire, education was only for a select few. Only boys were educated, and many of them lived too far from facilities to go to school at all. Most of the time, a boy's education was limited to some religious instruction rather than traditional schooling in subjects such as literature, history, or science. After the Republic of Turkey was formed, however, Atatürk insisted that everyone should go to school at the state's expense and receive a Western-style education. While primary and middle schools were formed, many religious schools were closed.

At first, all children were required to attend classes for five years, but in 1997, that requirement was increased to eight. Though the country now wants to educate all of its children, a few remain excluded. In 1986, 95 percent of primary school-aged children attended school.

Because the educational reforms begun by Atatürk are ongoing, children will be attending school for a longer period of time. Class sizes in Turkey are increasing and more teachers are needed. As an incentive for growth, Turkey is planning to increase teachers' salaries as well as change students' coursework by adding computer and foreign language classes.

Students stand in front of Atatürk's tomb in Ankara *(left)*. The design of the structure is similar to the Halicarnassus Mausoleum, one of the Seven Wonders of the World. Construction on Atatürk's mausoleum took place between 1944 and 1958. A metalsmith displays his wares in Ankara *(above)*. Recent excavations in Çayönü proved that the earliest signs of metalworking occurred more than 10,000 years ago.

In 1924, shortly after the Republic of Turkey was established, the Ministry of Education was officially appointed the task of opening Turkish schools and developing their curricula. This was an effort to bring the level of Turkish education in line with Western countries. Some of the goals of the Ministry are to ensure that Turkey has an adult population that is literate, knowledgeable about world affairs, and well trained in advancements in the sciences and in technology.

Although Turkey's youngest children can now receive optional preschool training in nursery schools and kindergartens, the percentage of those who actually attend classes remains small. In the early 1990s that number was 5.1 percent, though the government has a future goal of seeing at least 12 percent of preschool-aged children attending school.

By the age of six years, many Turkish children begin primary school, most dressed in a uniform. After five years, when they are eleven, children receive their primary school certificate and graduate to secondary school.

## Turkish Pride

Children in primary school attend a small ceremony every morning in which they shout out statements like, "I am a Turk. I am honest. I work hard." The children are expected to learn about Atatürk and to follow the principles of his revolution. Twice a week, on Monday and Friday, the children have a flag ceremony, where they sing the national anthem and raise the flag. In the spring, they develop school programs in which they sing songs, read poems, and perform in plays for an audience composed largely of their parents and teachers. The program marks the end of

Muslim students learn to interpret and memorize scripture at a Koranic school in Istanbul.

Turkish students participate in the physical education requirement of their curriculum studies. Primary education in Turkey consists of eight years and is compulsory and free at state schools.

their school year, which generally runs from September until May.

## Curriculum

The Turkish primary school curriculum is similar to that in the United States. Students are taught to read and write and to perform simple arithmetic functions. History and geography are also taught.

Secondary school education lasts for six years, although only three years are required. Many Turkish students begin learning English as soon as they reach secondary school, with many subjects such as math and science taught in English from that point forward.

Not all students receiving a secondary education take the same classes or are taught the same skills. Some high schools, called *lycées*, have an emphasis on teaching computer skills, science, or fine arts. Some lycées train future teachers. Most require students to learn at least one foreign language, often English or German. More than one lycée may be located within the same high school building.

A few lycées teach more specialized curricula like foreign trade and tourism. These schools are for children who want to work in the business or tourism industries. Some specialized schools also teach culinary skills. During the 1991–1992 school year, only 91 students attended lycées for culinary skills, while 5,236 studied the tourism industry, 582 studied foreign trade, and 226,864 learned about industry. Each lycée requires knowledge of academic subjects.

## Higher Education

The universities of Turkey are affiliated with the Higher Education Council, which was established in 1981. This council is authorized to administer the activities of all the institutions of higher learning in the country. The council oversees topics such as budgets,

evaluations, research, and planning and development. Besides universities, this body also oversees some high schools.

Since the establishment of the Republic of Turkey in 1923, founding and maintaining quality universities has been a priority for the government. Fifty-four new universities have been founded since that time. Students must take a two-phase examination to gain college placement. Some spend the entire year after high school graduation studying for their university entrance exams. Non-Turks who would like to study in Turkish universities may also take the entrance exams, which are given in both English and Turkish. If a foreign student earns a place at the university, he or she has one year to become proficient in Turkish before attending school in the country. During the 1991–1992 school year, more than 14,000 foreign students attended university at Turkish institutions.

Turkish universities are located across the country. Ankara has five and Istanbul three, though most other cities have only one. A few cities with universities are Bursa (Uludag University), Erzurum (Atatürk University), Konya (Seljuk University), Samsun (Ondokuz Mayis University), and Izmir (Dokuz Eylül University, Ege University, and Izmir High Technology University).

Many Turkish students study abroad, with many of them coming to the United States. The Web site of New York's Columbia University, for example, listed 120 Turkish Student Associations located on campuses within the United States in 2002. Many thousands of Turkish students then go on to work in the United States.

## Work

After graduation, most students enter the workforce. Because of the increased emphasis on industry, technology, and tourism, many become teachers, translators,

In this photograph, a farmer tills his field in Cappadocia. Because of Turkey's harsh climate, the production of grain and fruits in Turkey is limited; however, its many grasslands are ideal for raising cattle, sheep, and other livestock.

Turkish women are skilled in the ancient craft of carpet-weaving. Weavers use wool or silk thread and are aided by patterns to create the intricate designs. The Gallery Anatolia in Göreme receives funding to display the handmade carpets seen in this photograph.

engineers, or computer technicians. And as Turkey moves into the twenty-first century and attempts to align its business practices with what is acceptable for European Union membership, increasing numbers of students are needed in fields such as foreign trade and banking.

Most office workers in Turkey experience similar conditions to people in the United States with similar occupations. They normally work five days a week, from morning until early evening. Although many Turks do not get vacation time from their employers during their first year of employment, the country celebrates many national and religious holidays that provide time off to all workers.

Those who work outside of offices—in restaurants or hotels, for example—may work longer hours or during national holidays. Tourism is a growing industry in the country and an attractive career for many young people.

Many Turks, however, still work in more traditional fields such as farming. Turkey is an exporter of many citrus and nut crops as well as a producer of many

crops for consumption within the country. Most Turkish farmers own their acreage and their farms are relatively small compared with those in the United States. Besides vegetable and grain staples like rice, wheat, olives, almonds, oranges, and grapes, Turkish farmers also keep livestock like sheep and goats. The wool from both sheep and goats is highly prized.

Goats from the central region are of a breed called Angora. ("Angora" is another form of the word "Ankara," the name of the capital city.) These Angora goats produce very silky, fluffy wool.

Besides farming and raising livestock, other traditional jobs like fishing are still popular, sometimes with people whose families have been fishing along Turkish coasts for generations.

Relatively new occupations such as building, maintaining, and running railroads, highways, and airports are also important in a country that prides itself on following a Western model. All products—whether they are huge industrial machines, bales of hay, or crates of oranges—must be transported for export. This process often

This fish bazaar is a popular attraction in the Beyoglu district of Istanbul. Many restaurants in this section of the city serve authentically prepared Turkish seafood. This district is also known for the Tünel, the second oldest subway in Europe.

relies upon employees at various seaports, airports, train stations, or trucking companies.

## Turkey's Future

Like every nation, Turkey must find a way to balance its old traditions while incorporating new and more advanced methods of running its government and assisting its citizens. By reforming the school system and financing more buildings, more teachers, and more computers, Turkey looks to its future by educating its young people. By privatizing banks and by meeting the standards of the European Union, Turkey aligns itself with developed countries and attempts to ease its current economic difficulties. By establishing the Istanbul Stock Exchange, the country continues to integrate itself into the global financial market.

After the terrorist attacks of September 11, 2001, Turkey supported the United States's efforts to find the terrorists responsible, and was one of the countries that sent troops to Afghanistan. On the first anniversary of the attacks, the

Erdogan, the deputy leader of the Islamist-based Justice and Development Party (AK), was appointed in 2003. Since his term began, his agenda has been focused on strengthening Turkey's economy and gaining entrance into the European Union.

Turkish ambassador Osman Faruk Logoglu expressed his country's continued support of the United States. "Because we share the common values of freedom, democracy, and respect for human life, we stand by you now as we have done so many times in the past. Together, let us regard the anniversary of this horrific assault on freedom as cause to reaffirm our resilience in eradicating international terrorism."

Elections in 2002 brought a landslide victory to the Justice and Development Party. The party, which has wide acceptance among Islamists, immediately tried to calm international fears of a shift away from secular government. In March 2003, Recep Tayyip Erdogan was named Turkey's prime minister. "We will build a Turkey where common sense prevails," said party leader Erdogan, who was the former mayor of Istanbul. Erdogan pledged that his party would continue to pursue EU membership for Turkey and would remain a staunch supporter of the United States.

Turkey faces difficult times in the near future. The lira continues to lose value. Islamists continue to impose their values on Turkish society. Still, Turks can face their future with optimism. The reforms of Atatürk and his successors have established Turkey as an educated and dynamic nation that actively participates in world affairs. Turkey has a glorious past and, even if current conditions are rocky, Turks today can be proud of their country and optimistic about its future.

# TURKEY
## AT A GLANCE

## HISTORY

The earliest settlers in what is now Turkey were farmers thousands of years ago. Today we refer to them as Hittites. They were ruled by kings, and they buried their rulers in shaft tombs.

During the Bronze Age, Indo-Europeans moved into the area and formed the kingdom of the Hittites. Their capital was Hattusa. The Hittite kingdom survived for several centuries before environmental changes, new migrations of people from other areas, and a weakened government ended the reign of the Hittite kings.

Over the next several centuries, the Assyrians and Persians conquered the region. One king of this period remembered in history is Croesus, who ruled the kingdom of Lydia.

Alexander the Great defeated the Persians at the battle of Issus in 333 BC. Later, the Romans gained control of the area, and in 326, the eastern capital of the Roman Empire was established at Byzantium. The city was renamed Constantinople after the emperor Constantine I. The empire, though Roman in name, quickly became Greek in language and culture.

The Roman Empire in the west succumbed to various invasions, but the eastern leg of the empire survived. The Byzantines were besieged by Arabs, Slavs, Persians, and Seljuk Turks, but were not overthrown until AD 1453 when the Ottoman sultan Mehmed II bombarded the city's walls. After Mehmed captured the city, it was renamed Istanbul, which it remains today. Sultans also conquered much of southeast Europe, eventually reaching the city of Vienna under Süleyman the Magnificent.

The Ottoman Empire declined during the eighteenth and nineteenth centuries. Some sultans were little more than prisoners in their own palace. The situation was grim enough for others to refer to the empire as "the sick man of Europe."

However, after World War I, the Ottoman Empire was abolished. The Treaty of Lausanne drew internationally accepted borders for the new Republic of

Turkey, which was officially recognized in 1923. The sultan and his family were exiled and Mustafa Kemal, known as Atatürk became the new leader of Turkey. He instituted many reforms including the introduction of last names, giving women the right to vote, and changing the writing system from traditional Arabic script to Roman script.

Atatürk died in 1938. His successors have continued with reforms, though these have sometimes been sidetracked. The army has seized power and imposed martial law on several occasions. In 1982, a new constitution was drafted and martial law, imposed again in 1980, was gradually lifted.

Turkey was a charter member of the United Nations and is a member of NATO. Today, Turkey continues its quest for full membership into the European Union (EU).

## ECONOMY

Turkey's economy is the sixteenth largest in the world. The World Bank considers it one of the ten countries "most likely to enter the top tier of the world economy," while the U.S. Department of Commerce has declared Turkey to be one of the ten "most promising emerging economies."

During the 1980s, Turkey began a series of economic reforms to successfully integrate into the global economy. At the time, many banks and industries were controlled by the state. Today, this has largely changed. Some of the reforms were put in place to change import regulations while others were established in an effort to increase exports, encourage foreign capital investments, implement free-trade zones, and deregulate financial markets. As a result of these reforms, the Turkish economy grew at an average rate of 5 percent per year over the past two decades.

Although agriculture was once Turkey's main export, during the past twenty years the importance of agriculture has declined in favor of industrial exports. Today, Turkey's economy continues to shift from an agricultural to an industrial base.

The amount of Turkey's exports has increased from a level of $2.9 billion in 1980 to nearly $27 billion in 2000. Imports have also risen, from $7.9 billion in 1980 to almost $56 billion in 2000. Turkey's main exports are clothing and textiles, precious stones and minerals, iron and steel, and industrial machines such as boilers. Lately, more sophisticated technology such as motors, refrigerators, and even jet aircraft have been exported from Turkey. The nation also continues exporting agricultural products such as fruit, nuts, rice, and olive oil.

Privatization of previously state-controlled industries has also helped Turkey's economy. The government has completely withdrawn from many industries such as food processing and the production of cement. Banks are also being privatized.

One area of growth for the Turkish economy has been tourism. Although the industry dropped off slightly after the earthquakes in 1999, in 1998 more than nine million tourists visited the country and brought in more than $7 billion. The development of the tourist industry continues to be increasingly profitable.

In 1986, Turkey entered the global stock and bond markets through the establishment of the Istanbul Stock Exchange. Completely open to foreign investors, it was the best-performing stock exchange in the world by 1999.

Turkey had long petitioned to become a member of the European Union and had tried to get its laws and financial practices in line with requirements for membership. In December 1999, at the Helsinki Summit, Turkey was declared an official candidate for full membership. Because Turkey has familiarized itself over the years with the requests of full EU membership, the country will likely be granted membership status quickly.

All is not stable with Turkey's economy, however. High inflation and interest rates have been stumbling blocks in its attempt to create a healthy, diversified economy. The Turkish lira has also undergone a significant amount of devaluation. However, the Turkish government continues to work toward improving its overall economic forecast.

## GOVERNMENT AND POLITICS

The Republic of Turkey was founded on October 29, 1923. Although the country then had a constitution and a parliament and was supposed to be a democracy, power was reserved for Atatürk and his associates. In effect, Atatürk was a dictator. He used his power to enforce changes like the adoption of last names and use of the Roman alphabet, as well as improving the rights of women. Muslim courts and schools were closed and a secular (nonreligious) law code patterned after Switzerland's became the law of the land.

After World War II, Turkey became a charter member of the United Nations. The Republican People's Party decided to move the country into a more democratic style of government but was voted out of office during the elections of 1950. The Democrats led the country for ten years, but when people demonstrated against the government, the Democrats worked to restrain constitutional rights such as freedom of speech and freedom of the press.

The Turkish army seized control in 1960 and declared martial law. Democrat leaders were sent to jail. The army gave up control of the country within a year, however, and the general who had been in charge, Cemal Gürsel, resigned from the army and ran for president. He was elected.

The army took control of the government again in 1971 after the ruling Justice Party was unable to stop civilian violence. During the period of 1971–1980, the Justice Party and the Republican Party traded control of the country. The army once again took over and imposed martial law in 1980 under General Kenan Evren. A new constitution was drafted and voted on by Turks on November 6, 1982. The new constitution was approved by more than 90 percent of the voters. Martial law began to dissolve soon afterward, though its end did not come to all Turkish provinces until the late 1980s.

During the election of 1983, Turgut Ozal, a member of the Motherland Party, became prime minister. Eventually, Kenan Evren became president.

Turkey has had problems with its Kurdish minority for some time. The Kurds are not officially recognized as a minority, and so the government has not guaranteed their rights. In response, the Kurds formed the Kurdish Workers' Party (PKK) under Abdullah Ocalan. This militant group originally wanted independence but later changed its demand to an autonomous state within Turkey. An estimated thirty-five thousand people have died in battles between the PKK and the Turkish military. Ocalan was captured in 1999 and sentenced to death.

In 1974, Turkey invaded Cyprus after Turks and Greeks living on the island failed to resolve their internal disputes. Although a cease-fire was announced on August 16 of that year, Turkey remains in control of 40 percent of the island to this day. In 1975, the Turks living on Cyprus had formed their own state.

Since 1980, the government has decentralized much of its former power and has allowed privatization of banks and other industries to help it compete in the global marketplace.

# TIMELINE

**2300 BC**
Indo-Europeans move into Asia Minor

**1650 BC**
Labarna becomes first king of the Hittites

**715 BC**
Assyrians conquer Asia Minor

**1207 BC**
Last king of the Hittites, Suppiluliuma II, crowned

**1250 BC**
The Trojan War and the fall of Troy

**532–537**
Hagia Sophia built

**638–718**
Muslim Arabs besiege Constantinople

**1345**
Ottoman Turks gain first foothold in region at Gallipoli

**1453**
Sultan Mehmed II (the Conqueror) captures Constantinople, thereafter renamed Istanbul

**1974**
Turkey invades Cyprus

**1980**
Military coup begins three years of government under Martial Law

**1982**
New constitution approved

**1986**
Istanbul Stock Exchange opened

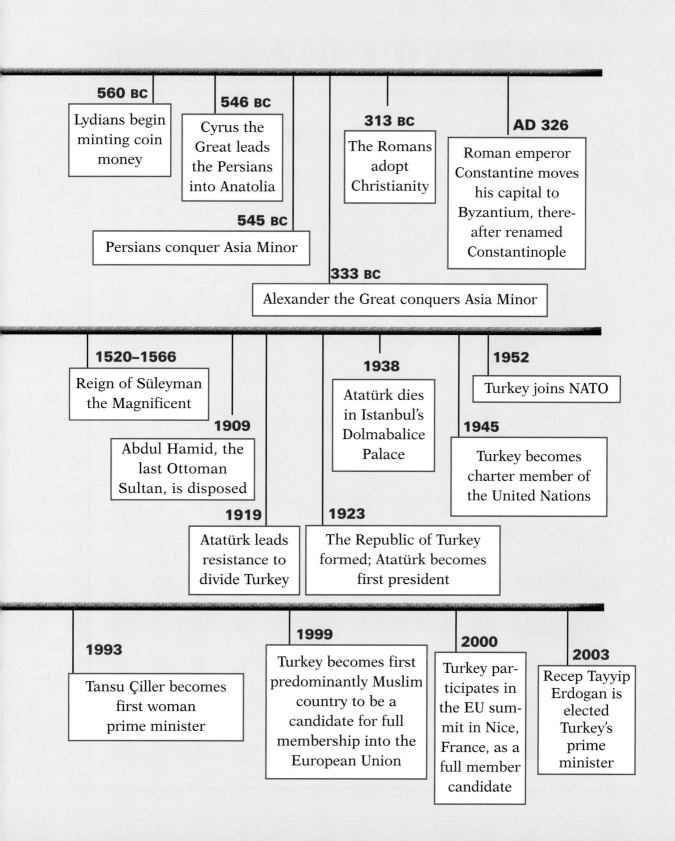

**560 BC**
Lydians begin minting coin money

**546 BC**
Cyrus the Great leads the Persians into Anatolia

**545 BC**
Persians conquer Asia Minor

**313 BC**
The Romans adopt Christianity

**AD 326**
Roman emperor Constantine moves his capital to Byzantium, thereafter renamed Constantinople

**333 BC**
Alexander the Great conquers Asia Minor

**1520–1566**
Reign of Süleyman the Magnificent

**1909**
Abdul Hamid, the last Ottoman Sultan, is disposed

**1938**
Atatürk dies in Istanbul's Dolmabalice Palace

**1952**
Turkey joins NATO

**1945**
Turkey becomes charter member of the United Nations

**1919**
Atatürk leads resistance to divide Turkey

**1923**
The Republic of Turkey formed; Atatürk becomes first president

**1993**
Tansu Çiller becomes first woman prime minister

**1999**
Turkey becomes first predominantly Muslim country to be a candidate for full membership into the European Union

**2000**
Turkey participates in the EU summit in Nice, France, as a full member candidate

**2003**
Recep Tayyip Erdogan is elected Turkey's prime minister

# TURKEY

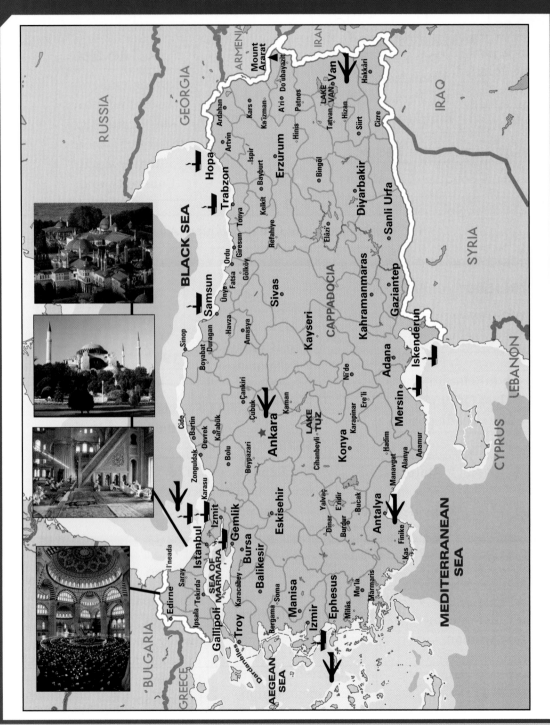

RUSSIA

GEORGIA

ARMENIA

IRAN

IRAQ

SYRIA

LEBANON

CYPRUS

BULGARIA

GREECE

BLACK SEA

Mount Ararat

Do'ubayazit

Kars
Ardahan
Arvin
Ispir
Bayburt
Kelkit
Refahiye
Erzurum
Bingöl
Elâzi
Diyarbakir
Sanli Urfa
Gaziantep

A'ri
Patnos
Van
LAKE VAN
Tatvan
Hizan
Siirt
Cizre
Hakkâri

Kaizman

Hopa
Trabzon
Tonya
Giresun
Ordu
Fatsa
Gökçöy
Ünye
Samsun
Havza
Amasya
Sinop
Boyabat
Duragan
Sivas
Kayseri
CAPPADOCIA
Kahramanmaras
Adana
Iskenderun
Mersin

Ni'de
Ere'li

Cide
Bartin
Devrek
Karabük
Zonguldak
Karasu
Izmit
Karacabey
Bolu
Beypazari
Çankiri
Çubuk
Kaman
Ankara
LAKE TUZ
Cihanbeyli
Karapinar
Konya
Hadim
Manavgat
Alanya
Anamur
Ardanmen
Erdemli

Istanbul
SEA OF MARMARA
Gemlik
Bursa
Eskisehir
Yalvaç
Dinar
Burdur
Er'dir
Bucak
Antalya
Finike
Kas

Edirne
Saray
Ipsala
Tekirda'
I'neada
Gallipoli
Troy
Dardanelles
Bergama
Soma
Manisa
Izmir
Ephesus
Milâs
Mu'la
Marmaris

AEGEAN SEA

MEDITERRANEAN SEA

Balikesir

# ECONOMIC FACT SHEET

**GDP in US$:** $444 billion

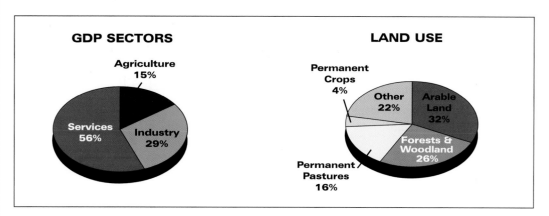

**Currency:** Turkish lira: 1,000,000 lira = $0.77 USD

**Workforce:** Agriculture 38%, services 38%, industry 24%

**Major Agricultural Products:** Tobacco, cotton, grain, olives, sugar beets, citrus

**Major Imports:** Machinery, chemicals, semifinished goods, fuels, transport equipment

**Major Exports:** Apparel, foodstuff, textiles, metal manufactures, transport equipment

**Significant Trading Partners:** Germany, United States, United Kingdom, Italy, France

**Rate of Unemployment:** Approximately 5.6%

**Average Income Per Capita:** $6,800

**Highways:** Total 229,235 m/382,059 km

**Railroads:** Total 5,164 m/8,607 km

**Waterways:** Total 720 m/1,200 km

**Airports:** 121

# POLITICAL FACT SHEET

**Official Name:** Republic of Turkey

**System of Government:**
Republican Parliamentary
Democracy, 1923

**Current President:**
Ahmet Necdet Sezer

**Current Prime Minister:**
Recep Tayyip Erdogan

**Federal Structure:**
Executive branch: president elected
by National Assembly for seven-

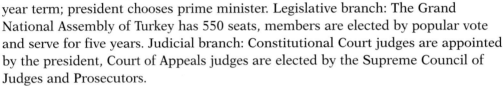

year term; president chooses prime minister. Legislative branch: The Grand
National Assembly of Turkey has 550 seats, members are elected by popular vote
and serve for five years. Judicial branch: Constitutional Court judges are appointed
by the president, Court of Appeals judges are elected by the Supreme Council of
Judges and Prosecutors.

**Number of Registered Voters:** 37,495,217

**Independence:** October 29, 1923

**Constitution:** November 7, 1982

**Legal System:** Derived from various European legal systems

**Suffrage:** Eighteen years of age; universal

**The Turkish National Anthem:**
The "Istiklal Marsi" (The Independence March) was officially adopted as Turkey's
national anthem. More than 700 poems were submitted to a competition organized to
select the most suitable composition. Finally, a poem by Mehmet Akif Ersoy was
unanimously approved by the Turkish Grand National Assembly in 1921.

*Fear not, the crimson flag, waving in these dawns will never fade*
*Before the last hearth that is burning in my nation vanishes.*
*That is my nation's star, it will shine;*
*That is mine, it belongs solely to my nation.*

*Oh coy crescent do not frown for I am ready to sacrifice myself for you!*
*Please smile upon my heroic nation, why that anger, why that rage?*
*If you frown, our blood shed for you will not be worthy.*
*Freedom is the right of my nation who worships God and seeks what is right.*

# CULTURAL FACT SHEET

**Official Language:** Turkish
**Major Religions:** 98% of the population is Muslim
**Capital:** Ankara
**Population:** 66,493,970
**Ethnic Groups:** 80% Turkish, 18% Kurdish, 2% others
**Life Expectancy:** Men 68 years, Women 73.2 years
**Time:** GMT +0200 (Daylight Savings: GMT +0300)
**Literacy Rate:** 81%
**National Flower:** Tulip
**Cultural Leaders:**

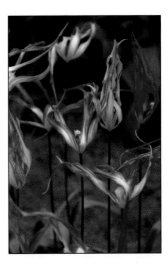

**Visual Arts:** Haluk Akakçe, J. Pascal Sebah, Fahrelnissa Zeid, Kutlug Ataman, Rifat Ozbek, Osman Hamdy-Bey

**Literature:** Gün Gencer, Murat Nemet-Nejat, Dervis Zaim, Halide Edip Adivar, Fazil Hüsnü Daglarca, Ihsani the Minstral, Orhan Veli Kanyk

**Music:** Fazil Say, Ali Ufki Bey, Seyfettin and Sezai Azal

**Entertainment:** Ahmet Ertegun, Ilhan Ersahin, Elia Kazan, Fatih Akin

**Sports:** Serap Aktas, Gülsün Durak, Naim Süleymanoglu, Halil Mutlu

---

## National Holidays and Festivals

As most Turkish holidays fall according to religious or non-standard calendars, the dates vary from year to year. The following list is in chronological order from January to December with firm dates included where applicable.

January 1: **New Year's Day**
**Seker Bayrami**    (Festival of the Breaking of the Fast)
**Kurban Bayrami**    (Feast of the Sacrifice)
March 21: **Kurdish New Year**
April 23: **National Independence and Children's Day** (Anniversary of the first Grand National Assembly)

May 19: **Youth Day**
August 30: **Victory Day**
October 29: **Republic Day** (Declaration of the Turkish Republic)
November 10: **The Anniversary of Atatürk's Death**

# GLOSSARY

**börek (BURR-ik)** A sweet pastry.

**dervish (DUR-vish)** A member of a mystical form of Islam where dancing is part of one's spiritual growth.

**harem (HAAR-em)** The women's quarters of a house.

**Islam (IS-lam)** The religion of the Muslims, which includes belief in Allah as the sole deity and Muhammad as his prophet.

**kiosk (KEE-osk)** An open pavilion.

**madrasa (muh-druh-SUH)** A religious school of Islam.

**mosque (MAHSK)** A building used for public worship by Muslims.

**Muhammad (ma-HAM-mud)** The Islamic prophet who delivered the religious stories that make up the Koran.

**Muslim (MUZ-lim)** A follower of Islam.

**Osman (ohs-MAN)** The founder of the Ottoman ruling dynasty.

**Osmanli (ohs-MAN-lee)** A different name for the Turkish language.

**Ottomans (AH-tuh-menz)** The Turks who ruled Turkey after the fall of the Seljuk Empire.

**pilav (pee-LUV)** A rice dish; often spelled "pilaf" in English.

**Koran (koo-RAN)** A book composed of sacred writings accepted by Muslims as revelations made to Muhammad by Allah.

**Ramazan (RA-muh-zan)** The Muslim month of fasting; often spelled "Ramadan" in other countries.

**Seljuk (SEL-juhk)** The first Turks to rule Turkey.

**Shiite (SHEE-ite)** A Muslim of the branch of Islam that believes their leaders should be descendants of Muhammad.

**simik (SIM-ehk)** A bread ring sold by street vendors.

**sultan (SUHL-tan)** A ruler of the Ottoman Empire.

**Sunni (SOON-nee)** A Muslim of the branch of Islam that accepts Abu Bakr as first caliph.

**yali (YUH-lee)** A waterfront house on the Bosporus Strait.

# FOR MORE INFORMATION

Turkish Embassy in the United States
O. Faruk Logoglu, Ambassador
2525 Massachusetts Avenue NW
Washington, DC 20008
Web site: http://www.turkey.org

United States Embassy in Turkey
W. Robert Pearson, Ambassador
110 Ataturk Boulevard
Kavaklidere, 06100 Ankara
Turkey
Web site: http://www.usemb-ankara.org.tr

## Web Sites

Due to the changing nature of Internet links, the Rosen Publishing Group, Inc., has developed an online list of Web sites related to the subject of this book. This site is updated regularly. Please use this link to access the list:

http://www.rosenlinks.com/pswc/turk

# FOR FURTHER READING

Bagdasarian, Adam. *Forgotten Fire*. London: DK Publishing, 2000.

Bator, Robert. *Daily Life in Ancient and Modern Istanbul* (Cities Through Time). Minneapolis: Lerner Publications Company, 2000.

Hoyt-Goldsmith, Diane. *Celebrating Ramadan: Ramadan Al-Muazzam*. New York: Holiday House, 2001.

Kemal, Neriman. *Turkey* (Countries of the World). Milwaukee: Gareth Stevens, 2002.

Khan, Rukhsana. *Muslim Child: Understanding Islam Through Stories and Poems*. Morton Grove, IL: Albert Whitman & Co., 2002.

Miller, Louise R. *Turkey: Between East & West* (Exploring Cultures of the World). Tarrytown, NY: Benchmark Books, 1998.

Penney, Sue. *Islam* (World Beliefs and Cultures). Crystal Lake, IL: Heinemann Library, 2001.

Wagner, Heather Lehr. *Turkey* (Creation of the Modern Middle East). Philadelphia, Chelsea House, 2002.

# BIBLIOGRAPHY

Bassiouni, M. Cherif. *Introduction to Islam*. Chicago: Rand McNally & Company, 1988.

Bryce, Trevor. *The Kingdom of the Hittites*. Oxford, England: Oxford University Press, 1998.

Bulfinch, Thomas. *The Age of Fable*. New York: Mentor Classics, 1962.

Ceram, C.W. *The Secret of the Hittites*. London: Phoenix Press, 1956.

Central Intelligence Agency. "Turkey." Retrieved April 5, 2002 (http://www.cia.gov/cia/publications/factbook/geos/tu.html).

Columbia University. "Turkey at a Glance." Retrieved April 4, 2002 (http://www.columbia.edu/~sss31/Turkiye/gov-system.html and http://www.columbia.edu/~sss31/Turkiye/edu.html).

Ekrem, Selma. *Turkish Fairy Tales*. Princeton, NJ: D. Van Nostrand Company, Inc., 1964.

Encyclopedia.com. "Uralic and Altaic Languages." Retrieved March 13, 2002 (http://www.encyclopedia.com/articls/13269.html).

Engels, Donald W. *Alexander the Great and the Logistics of the Macedonian Army*. Berkeley, CA: University of California Press, 1978.

Fuller, J. F. C. *The Generalship of Alexander the Great*. New Brunswick, NJ: Da Capo Press, 1960.

Greatbuildings.com. "Hagia Sophia." Retrieved March 19, 2002 (http://www.greatbuildings.com/buildings/Hagia_Sophia.html).

Guidetoturkey.com. "Flora & Fauna." Retrieved March 18, 2002 (http://www.guidetoturkey.com/aboutturkey/info_tips/flora_fauna.asp).

Hellier, Chris. *Splendors of Istanbul: Houses and Palaces along the Bosporus*. New York: Abbeville Press Publishers, 1993.

Howe, Marvine. *Turkey Today: A Nation Divided over Islam's Revival*. Boulder, CO: Westview Press, 2000.

Lewis, Bernard. *The Emergence of Modern Turkey*, second edition. London: Oxford University Press, 1968.

Martinovitch, Nicholas N. *The Turkish Theatre*. New York: Benjamin Blom, 1968.

Mitler, Louis. *Contemporary Turkish Writers*. Bloomington, IN: Indiana University, 1988.

Norwich, John Julius. *Byzantium: The Early Centuries*. New York: Alfred A. Knopf, 1989.

Pope, Hugh, and Nicole Pope. *Turkey Unveiled*. New York: The Overlook Press, 1997.

Rice, David Talbot. *The Art of Byzantium*. New York: Harry N. Abrams Inc., 1959.

Ruthven, Malise. *Islam: A Very Short Introduction*. Oxford, England: Oxford University Press, 1997.

Stierlin, Henri. *Turkey: From the Selçuks to the Ottomans*. New York: Taschen, 1998.

Tierney, Brian, and Sidney Painter. *Western Europe in the Middle Ages 300–1475*. New York: Alfred A. Knopf, Inc., 1983.

Turkish Embassy. "Recent Developments in the Turkish Economy." Retrieved March 19, 2002 (http://www.turkey.org/business/turkish-ec.htm).

Turizm.net. "Education." Retrieved April 4, 2002 (http://www.turizm.net/turkey/info/education.html).

Valent, Dani. *World Food: Turkey*. Victoria, Australia: Lonely Planet Publications Pty. Ltd., 2000.

Walker, Barbara K. *Art of the Turkish Tale*, Vol. 1 and 2. Lubbock, TX: Texas Tech University Press, 1993.

# PRIMARY SOURCE IMAGE LIST

**Page 6:** This contemporary photograph was taken by Eitan Simanor and shows the ancient Roman city of Ephesus. Once surrounded by a colonnade and shops, this path is known as the Sacred Way.

**Page 7:** Pictured in this contemporary photo is the seventeenth-century Sultanahmet Mosque, also known as the Blue Mosque in Istanbul, Turkey. It was built by the Ottoman architect Sedefkar Mehmet Agha and has six minarets.

**Page 8:** This contemporary photo taken by Jeffrey Alford features the coast of the Black Sea and was taken in Trabzon, Turkey.

**Page 11:** These "fairy chimneys" in Cappadocia, Turkey, look much like they did when they were designed between the fourth through the fourteenth centuries. This is a photograph of the landscape in present-day Cappadocia.

**Page 13:** The Karanlik Kilise, or "Dark Church," part of Göreme Open Museum, was built in Cappadocia, Turkey, in the eleventh century. Its medieval Byzantine-styled features are still noticeable in this contemporary photograph.

**Page 15:** R.S. Michaud took this contemporary photograph of the Black Sea.

**Page 16:** This modern photograph of Mt. Ararat, Turkey's highest peak, was taken by Fred Maroon. The peak of Mt. Ararat is considered by some to be the biblical resting place of Noah's ark.

**Page 20:** A contemporary photograph taken of the present-day view from the citadel in Ankara, Turkey.

**Page 22:** The manuscript illumination pictured on this page dates from the fifteenth century. It is part of the Medieval Collection of the Biblioteque Nationale in Paris, France.

**Page 23:** This contemporary photograph was taken in modern Bogazkoy, Turkey, in 1980.

**Page 24:** The Hittite bas-relief of a noble pictured on this page was discovered in Karatepe. It dates from the mid-eighth century BC.

**Page 25:** Originally printed in *Harper's Weekly* on January 23, 1875, these drawings were made of Heinrich Schliemann's discovery of the ancient city of Troy. Schliemann, a German-born amateur archaeologist began digging on the site of his discovery in 1865. It is now located in present-day Hisarlik, Turkey.

**Page 26 (top):** This modern photograph features the world's oldest known peace treaty between the Egyptians and the Hittites and is dated 1269 BC. It is currently located in the Archaeological Museum in Istanbul, Turkey,

**Page 26 (bottom):** This fifth-century Greek vase depicts the Battle of Troy.

**Page 27:** Currently a part of the permanent collection of the Louvre Museum in Paris, this Greek vase by Myson depicts King Croesus on his funeral pyre and dates from 500 to 490 BC.

**Page 28 (top):** This statue of Constantine I celebrates the Roman emperor at the time he was proclaimed governor in AD 306. It is located in York, England.

**Page 28 (bottom):** Pictured on this page is a fifteenth-century Ottoman watercolor painting of the Sultan Fatih Mehmed II. It is currently housed in the Topkapi Palace Museum in Istanbul, Turkey.

**Page 29 (top):** This painting of the 1453 siege of Constantinople was completed in 1537 and is currently housed at the Monastery of Moldovita in Romania.

**Page 29 (bottom):** This eleventh-century manuscript illustrating the battle between the Byzantines and the Seljuks is one of 574 pages of the *Synopsis Historiarum*. It is currently housed in the Biblioteca Nacional in Madrid, Spain.

**Page 30:** This copper engraving by A. Mallet was done between 1683 and 1686 and features Janissaries during the Ottoman period in Turkey.

**Page 31:** Sir John Tenniel drew this political cartoon entitled "Tightening the Grip" in 1877.

**Page 32 (top):** This 1923 photograph of dignitaries signing the Treaty of Lausanne was taken on July 16 in Lausanne, Switzerland.

**Page 32 (bottom):** This early photograph of Mustafa Kemal, known as Atatürk, was provided by the Turkish Embassy in Istanbul, Turkey.

**Page 33:** Jeffrey Alfred, a photographer for the Associated Press Agency took this modern photograph of Kurdish Nomads near Lake Van in Turkey.

**Page 34:** Taken in Kyrenia, Cyprus, this 1974 photograph of Turkish troops landing on the island was shot on the first day of the Turkish invasion.

**Page 35:** This photograph of Kurdish Workers' Party (PKK) demonstrators taken in Strasburg, France, shows a flag featuring the Kurdish rebel leader Abdullah Ocalan, who was jailed by Turkish authorities but later freed in 1998.

**Page 36:** This manuscript page, dated 1558, is entitled "Sultan Süleyman the Magnificent Hunting in Western Anatolia" and is from *Süleymanname*, or *The Book of Süleyman*, the sixteenth-century Ottoman sultan. The entire manuscript is currently a part of the permanent collection of the Topkapi Palace Museum in Istanbul, Turkey.

**Page 37:** The Koranic inscription pictured on this page says, "In the name of God, the compassionate and holy one" and is located on a mosque in Istanbul, Turkey.

**Page 38 (top):** The detail of the Greek column pictured on this page was once a part of the ruins of Troy and was found in the north Aegean part of Turkey.

**Page 38 (bottom):** This illustrated manuscript page dates from AD 1250 and is an illustration of the poem "The Romance of Varqa and Gulshah." It was painted by Abd al Mu'min al Khayyam and is currently housed in the Topkapi Palace Museum in Istanbul, Turkey.

**Page 39 (bottom):** Part of an illustrated Islamic manuscript that dates as far back as the fourteenth century, this folio features mamluk slave warriors. It is a part of the collection of the Pierpont Morgan Library in New York, New York.

**Page 40:** Part of the Hunername manuscript, this folio features the military campaigns of Süleyman the Magnificent and is located at the Topkapi Palace Museum in Istanbul, Turkey.

**Page 43:** Atatürk is seen in this photograph teaching children the Latin alphabet during his tenure as president of Turkey (1923–1938). This photograph was provided by the Turkish Embassy in Istanbul, Turkey.

**Page 44:** The ancient shrine pictured in this contemporary photograph shows the scene atop Mount Nemrut where numerous sculptures were placed around the first century BC. Once a part of northern Mesopotamia, this area is currently a section of central Anatolia, Turkey.

**Page 48:** This third-century Roman mosaic depicting Ulysses was found at the site known as Thugga, located in present-day Tunisia. It is currently housed in the Musee du Bardo, in Bardo, Tunisia.

**Page 54:** This contemporary photograph of high school students celebrating Turkey's national Youth and Sports Day was taken on May 19, 2001.

**Page 59:** These Turkish air force officers are celebrating Victory Day ceremonies in August 1999 at the Mausoleum of Atatürk in Ankara, Turkey.

**Page 62:** This folio of a medieval Koran is part of the permanent collection of the Musee Conde in Chantilly, France.

**Page 67:** The sixteenth-century miniature found on this page depicts whirling dervishes as they might have appeared during the Middle Ages. It is now located in the Topkapi Sarayi Library in Istanbul, Turkey.

**Page 72:** The Iznik tiles featured in this photo can be found in the circumcision room in the Topkapi Palace Museum in Istanbul, Turkey.

**Page 75:** Yann Arthus Bertrand took this aerial photograph of Istanbul's Topkapi Palace in 1997.

**Page 77:** Built by Count Ostrorog, this 1996 photograph of Turkey's famous Ostrorog yali was taken by Chris Heller in 1996 from the Bosporus waterfront.

**Page 78:** A theatrical performance in a former Ottoman textile factory located in Istanbul, Turkey, caught by a photographer in 2000.

**Page 79:** These master puppeteers were photographed during a performance in Istanbul in 2000.

**Page 80:** Topkapi Palace Museum is the place to view this Turkish miniature painting dated 1610 that features a festival of court musicians.

**Page 82:** This folio from the Codex Justinianus features an early version of Roman laws. It dates from AD 528 and may currently be found in the Biblioteca Capitolare in Verona, Italy.

**Page 84:** This photograph of Orhan Veli Kanik dates from the 1950s.

**Page 85:** Mustafa Kemal (Atatürk) is featured in this photo alongside the poet Halide Edip Adivar and was taken sometime during the 1940s or 1950s.

**Page 86:** This photograph of Fazil Hüsnü Daglarca dates from the 1970s.

**Page 87:** Burhan Ozbilici took this photograph for the Associated Press Agency in 1997 of a musician near the Galata Bridge and Yeni Camii Mosque in Istanbul.

**Page 88:** Murad Sezer took this photograph in Istanbul for the Associated Press Agency in 1998 during the month-long celebration of Ramadan.

**Page 90:** This contemporary photograph features a family of Kurds pounding bulgur wheat.

**Page 95:** Burhan Ozbilici took this photograph for the Associated Press Agency of this Istanbul street vendor selling bread rings.

**Page 100:** Wrestling festivals like the one in this photograph take place every year in Edirne, Turkey. This photograph was taken by Jeffrey L. Rotman during the Kirkpinar Festival in July 1996.

**Page 101:** A cirit player on horseback is the subject of this contemporary photograph taken in Istanbul, Turkey.

**Page 104:** An Islamic primary school captured by photographer David Rubinger in Istanbul, Turkey, in 1987.

**Page 105:** Turkish children enjoy daily activities as a part of their busy school day as seen in this photograph by Staffan Widstrand taken in Antalya, Turkey, in 1990.

**Page 107:** Richard T. Nowitz took this photograph of a farmer in Cappadocia in 1988.

**Page 109:** Roberto Arakaki captured this image of a fish market in the Beyoglu District in Istanbul, Turkey.

**Page 110:** Eyal Warshavsky took this photograph of the Istanbul Stock Exchange on August 26, 1999.

# INDEX

127

# Turkey: A Primary Source Cultural Guide

## About the Author

Martha Kneib is a native St. Louisan who holds a master's degree in anthropology. She devotes most of her time to writing, maintaining her Web sites, and traveling with her husband. This is her third book for the Rosen Publishing Group.

**Designer:** Geri Giordano; **Cover Designer:** Tahara Hasan; **Editor:** Joann Jovinelly;
**Photo Researcher:** Gillian Harper